THE LOST CIVILIZATION: THE STORY OF THE CLASSIC MAYA

HARPER'S CASE STUDIES IN ARCHAEOLOGY

William A. Longacre,
General Editor

THE LOST CIVILIZATION: THE STORY OF THE CLASSIC MAYA

T. PATRICK CULBERT

University of Arizona

HARPER & ROW, PUBLISHERS

New York, Evanston, San Francisco, London

Cover photograph courtesy of John A. Graham,
University of California, Berkeley.

Sponsoring Editor: Walter H. Lippincott
Project Editor: Elizabeth Dilernia
Production Supervisor: Valerie Klima

THE LOST CIVILIZATION:
THE STORY OF THE
CLASSIC MAYA

Library of Congress Cataloging in Publication Data
Culbert, T. Patrick.
The lost civilization: the story of the classic Maya.

(Harper's case studies in archaeology)
1. Mayas—Antiquities. 2. Mayas—History.
3. Central America—Antiquities. I. Title.
F1435.C82   970.3   73-10683
ISBN 0-06-041448-0

CONTENTS

EDITOR'S FOREWORD

As student interest in anthropology and archaeology has increased in recent years, I have seen a need for a series of supplementary texts such as "Harper's Case Studies in Archaeology." The rapid growth of enrollments in introductory courses and the offering of such courses in ever larger numbers of colleges and universities across the country have placed a considerable strain on the relatively meager resources available, particularly those used in the teaching of archaeology. My concern over the lack of teaching resources in archaeology is shared by many in the profession. I am grateful not only for the positive response to the idea of a series of short monographs reporting problem-oriented archaeological research but also for the commitment of scholars to produce exciting accounts of their current research.

The books in this series are designed to show the methods by which archaeologists solve research problems of broad anthropological significance. The range of problems, time periods, and areas of the world studied has been selected to provide maximum utility and flexibility for the teachers of introductory anthropology and archaeology courses. The series will provide an integrated set of monographs that introduce the student to basic aspects of modern archaeological research. There is probably no more effective means to convey the excitement and relevance of modern, problem-oriented archaeological investigation than to have the investigators who conceive and carry out such research prepare the monographs themselves. By providing an integrated view of the most recent directions in archaeological research, the monographs will challenge the instructor to put recent investigations into historical perspective and encourage the student to develop an appreciation of the importance of the development of anthropological archaeology in light of the present thrust of our discipline. The student will also share in the current emphasis upon relevant research designed to reveal the nature of cultural evolution. The emphasis of the series is explicitly upon process—processes of change and stability in the development of culture. As such, the series is designed to contribute to the teaching of modern anthropology and to emphasize the important role that archaeological research plays in achieving the larger goals of anthropology.

THE AUTHOR AND HIS BOOK

T. Patrick Culbert is Associate Professor of Anthropology at the University of Arizona in Tucson. He received the Doctor of Philosophy degree in anthropology from the University of Chicago in 1962. Before joining the faculty of the University of Arizona in 1964, Professor Culbert taught at the University of Mississippi and Southern Illinois University, and he was a Visiting Professor at the Universidad de San Carlos in Guatemala.

His professional interests and research have been focused upon the Maya civilization in Mesoamerica. Since 1961 he has been in charge of the analysis of ceramics recovered from the Maya site of Tikal in Guatemala in the important excavations being conducted there by the University of Pennsylvania. He has just completed a major professional report on the ceramics of Tikal that will be published as one of the series of Tikal Reports by the University Museum at the University of Pennsylvania.

Among the major problems of the Maya yet to be solved by archaeologists is the collapse of that civilization during the Classic Period more than 1000 years ago. Interest in the Maya collapse led Professor Culbert to organize and chair an Advanced Seminar for the School of American Research in Santa Fe, New Mexico, devoted to an exploration of the factors responsible for the disintegration of the Maya civilization. This seminar resulted in an important new synthesis and concomitant new understanding of the collapse. The interested student is urged to read the resulting book, *The Classic Maya Collapse*, that Professor Culbert edited for the University of New Mexico Press (1973).

Perhaps no prehistoric development in the New World has attracted as much interest or has been surrounded with more mystery in the popular press as the emergence and disappearance of the Maya civilization in Mesoamerica. This book skillfully provides us with an up-to-date synthesis of that civilization.

As such, it represents one of the end-products of archaeological research, a descriptive historical narrative of a viable culture that existed in the past.

It also uses the Maya civilization as a case study for the exploration of processes of cultural stability and change in cross-cultural perspective. Using the Maya as one example of that type of complex society anthropologists call civilization permits important perspective for the understanding and solution of problems that confront our own version of civilization today. The reader will discover, for example, that the problems of "over-population" or an "energy crisis" are not novel or restricted to our own era. Indeed, an understanding of these general pressures in the rise and fall of the Maya civilization might well help us to achieve a more rational solution for these pressing problems in today's world.

William A. Longacre

INTRODUCTION

Civilizations are those relatively rare human societies that achieve unusually high degrees of cultural complexity. The anthropologist, engaged in unraveling the workings of human cultures, must deal with these complex systems, and in dealing with them he faces his most difficult, most challenging, and most urgent task. We ourselves, of course, are part of a civilization. In fact, though in nostaligc moments we might wish it otherwise, civilization is rapidly becoming inescapable for the inhabitants of our entire planet. We have also realized, with the suddenness of a revelation, that the patterns of growth that are inherent properties of civilizations do not necessarily lead to creating a better life but may instead point inexorably toward overpopulation, overexploitation of the environment, and eventual destruction. We begin to suspect, then, that understanding the workings of complex cultural systems may be more pressing than the harmless and mildly irrelevant pastime it seemed not long ago. This is the field in which anthropologists, economists, historians, and a host of other students of our culture meet with different viewpoints of the same, almost incredibly complex, phenomenon. Like the blind man with the elephant, we must decide on the nature of the beast we have all been observing.

The questions that the anthropologist asks of civilizations are myriad. What are the conditions, apparently quite rare, that cause some cultures to take the step to civilization? Are the properties of civilizations those common to all human cultures but "writ large," or are totally new *kinds* of organizations generated with increased complexity? What are the limits that the environment places on individual civilizations, and how do the civilizations strike and maintain an equilibrium within those limits? What governs the interaction between civilizations and determines whether the interaction will be peaceful or hostile? What leads to the periods of decline or collapse that have been the fate of all earlier civilizations? These questions must be answered comparatively by analyses of features common to a series of civilizations. The strength of anthropology is in providing, by its eclectic emphasis upon a multiplicity of cultures, the basis for comparison. The anthropologist can see the processes of civilization at work not once, but several times under different circumstances.

The purpose of this book is not to answer the general comparative questions about civilization that are our ultimate concern, but to examine a particular case of civilization—that of the Maya of lowland Guatemala and British Honduras.

Perhaps of all the New World civilizations the Maya civilization is surrounded by the greatest aura of mystery and most vividly generates the excitement of the unknown and exotic. This is in part a result of the circumstances of its discovery. The Maya centers were about as close as one can get to being a "lost civilization," the ruins of which, covered by a millennium of rain forest growth and decay, lay forgotten and generally unknown. In the 1840s, the immensely popular travel accounts of John Lyoyd Stevens and the enchanting drawings of Frederick Catherwood brought the Maya to the romantic imagination of mid-nineteenth century America. The setting of Maya civilization contributed to the romance, since tropical rain forest is so far outside the experience of most North Americans that they might expect almost anything to flourish therein. That the Maya were undeniably intellectuals who left behind an undeciphered script holding unknown and unimaginable secrets deepened the air of mystery. Finally, the fact that their descendants at the time of the Conquest, unlike the Aztecs and Incas, bore little obvious connection with the ancient centers freed the imagination from the specter of a very real people who fought and died and proved inadequate to cope with the impinging European cultures.

The romanticism of a century ago has faded in the face of the pragmatic scientism of the last two generations. Yet in some ways the puzzle of the Maya has continued. The principles that seem to operate well in explaining most early civilizations sit very uneasily upon the Maya. According to these principles, the Maya should not have thrived in a tropical rain forest environment. They should not have been able to congregate thousands of people in the service of vast ceremonial centers. The lower classes, upon which any civilization rests, should not have been willing to contribute such quantities of labor and goods for the preservation of a system that seemed to offer them little reward. And yet these things undeniably happened and the Maya flourished for more than a millennium as one of the great civilizations of antiqiuity. Finally, Maya Classic culture collapsed so utterly that a large part of the territory it occupied remains unpopulated to the present day. Although the fall of civilizations is a commonplace event in history, a devastation so complete and lasting as that which afflicted the Maya area is very unusual, and the failure of Maya culture to reconstitute itself must be explained. There is justification, then, for saying that Maya mysteries remain and that the workings of Maya culture have proved even more resistant to explanations than those of the most early civilizations.

I find this is a particularly exciting moment in the history of Maya studies to write this book, because I feel that we are on the threshold of a new understanding that should erase some of the problems in the old ways of looking at Maya Classic culture. In October 1970, eleven scholars gathered at Santa Fe, New Mexico, to attend a conference sponsored by the School of American Research to reconsider the question of the collapse of Classic Maya civilization. For a week we argued, cajoled, tested each other's ideas, and tried to make sense out of a situation for which no previous explanation had proved satisfactory. It soon became apparent that we could not understand the Maya collapse until we knew what sort of civilization had collapsed. This discovery forced us back to beginnings—to a painful reexamination of premises about the Maya that had been generally accepted for many years. All of us had been uneasy about some of these premises and about features of the standard reconstruction of the way Maya society worked, and all of us had bits and pieces of alternative reconstructions. Within a week of work, these bits and pieces began to fit and new ways of understanding began to emerge. These results are not the final answer to either the nature of Maya society or the reasons for its fall. They provide, however, a new model that can be tested in the field where all ideas must stand or fall in the light of data. What I will present in this book is my present understanding of what made Classic Maya society work. I am not satisfied with it, but I am pleased with it as a start toward a more coherent system that will in the long run be testable and that can lead us closer than before to the real workings of Maya culture.

T. P. C.

1. The Setting of Maya Civilization

The continent of North America narrows, funnel-like, at its southern end and empties across the Isthmus of Panama into South America not far from where Balboa stood "silent upon a peak in Darien." Some 800 miles to the northwest of the Isthmus, the narrowing of the continent is interrupted by the Yucatan Peninsula, which projects northward like a giant thumb from the chain of volcanic mountains that parallel the Pacific coast. At this point in the continent the Pacific coast runs almost east–west rather than its familiar north–south, so that in traveling due north from the Pacific coast of Guatemala one would bisect the Yucatan Peninsula and cross the United States on a line passing close to New Orleans and Chicago. In fact, for those who are enchanted by little-known facts of no particular utility, it might be noted that to reach the Pacific Ocean from Chicago it is closer to go to the Pacific coast of Guatemala than to any part of the coast in the United States.

The Yucatan Peninsula (Figure 1) is a limestone platform 80,000 square miles in extent. Geologically, the northern half of the peninsula has only recently risen from the sea, while the southern half has alternated between being a part of North America and a part of a now-vanished "Caribbean Land" that included the Greater Antilles and extensive parts of what is now the southern Caribbean Sea. For our purposes, however, the history of the Yucatan Peninsula is an eternity and, for the few thousand years with which we are concerned, the topography and climate of the peninsula were always much the same as they are today.

It was in the forests of the Yucatan Peninsula and in the neighboring verdant mountains of Guatemala and of Chiapas, Mexico, that the Maya built their civilization. It is here also that their modern descendants live, a vigorous and independent people, but one reduced to the status of tribal enclaves and marginal participants in modern Western culture. The term ['Maya" most properly refers to a family of languages separated

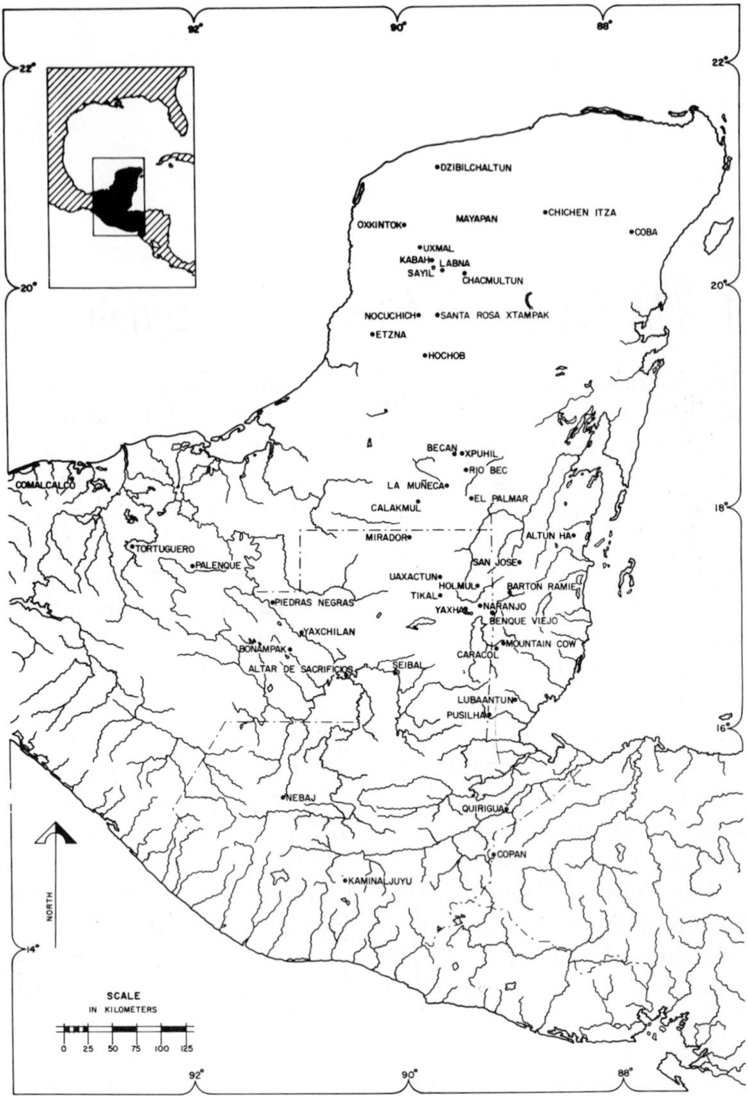

Figure 1

Map of the Maya Area. (*University of New Mexico Press.*)

from each other by about the same order of difference that separates the Romance languages. The continuous distribution of Maya languages, the gradual variations between them, and the lack of other languages in the area lead to an inescapable conclusion that Maya speakers have inhabited the same area for a long time. Consequently we can feel confident that the prehistoric inhabitants of the area were also Maya speakers. However, it is only a part of the prehistoric Maya that will concern us. To reconstruct in a few pages the lifeways in even the best-known parts of the Maya realm is a Herculean task that only the incurably optimistic would attempt. To complicate the job by introducing problems of regional diversity would simply add pages of ifs, buts, and maybes, each followed by the solemn pronouncement that we cannot answer the questions with the evidence presently available.

The focus of the book, then, is on the Maya who lived a thousand and more years ago in the southern half of the Yucatan Peninsula. Such a focus eschews a consideration of the prehistoric inhabitants of the Maya highlands, the mountain massifs of Guatemala and Chiapas. But the cultural history of the highland areas differs notably from that of the lowland areas and may justifiably be reserved as a separate problem worthy of treatment in its own right. This focus also avoids a consideration of prehistoric Maya culture of the lowlands in the northern half of the Yucatan Peninsula. This exclusion is not so easily defensible as the exclusion of the highlands for it could be forcefully argued that the whole Maya lowlands make an interconnected unit. I am led to my decision, however, by the unavoidable admission that much of what I might say about the northern lowlands would have to be invented by extending patterns well known in the south to cover fragmentary, and sometimes quite unclear, facts from the north. I shall, then, stick to the area I know best, secure in the knowledge that even there more than enough opportunity exists to stretch scanty data into venturesome interpretations.

Henceforth, I will refer to our area of primary interest as either the southern Maya lowlands or the Peten, after the district of Guatemala the Maya occupied. Actually, to use the term "Peten" for the Maya heartland is somewhat inaccurate since the zone of Maya sites also includes most of Belize (British Honduras) to the east and a narrow fringe of southern Mexico to the west. But Peten is a short and pleasing word, sanctified by generations of usage by archaeologists, and I will be happy to perpetuate it in all its inaccuracy.

Most of the southern lowlands is a limestone plateau lying only 300 to 700 feet above sea level. To describe the Peten as a plateau, however, conjures up images of a flat and featureless plain. Only one who has cursed and sweated up Peten hills in 90-degree heat and comparable humidity can truly appreciate how mistaken such an image is. Actually the region consists of

a series of steep limestone ridges one or two hundred feet high
from base to top (Figure 2). These ridges have an effect on living
conditions quite out of proportion to their size. The tops and
sides of the ridges are the only land suitable for occupation.
Here the land is well drained and the water has a chance to run
off during rainy season. The troughs between ridges, on the
other hand, collect water during rains, and, although dry land
most of the year, the troughs become seasonal swamps called
bajos during the rainy months. The absence of ruins in *bajos*
suggests that the prehistoric Maya avoided these areas as studiously as do the inhabitants of today.

The only major topographic feature that rises above the
general level of the southern lowlands is the Maya Mountains,
a low range of ancient volcanic origin that occupies the southern
part of Belize. Because of the nature of the soil, the Maya Mountains are covered with extensive pine forests, a striking anomaly
at the low elevations that they reach (1000 to 3000 feet).

Figure 2

Tikal and the Rain Forest. *This view, looking northward across the
main ceremonial center at Tikal, gives a perspective of the rain forest
and the limestone ridge country of the Peten District of Guatemala.
(The University Museum, University of Pennsylvania.)*

Although unattractive for agriculture and occupation, the mountains offered a source of volcanic stone that was greatly prized by the Maya in their limestone wilderness.

Most of the Peten acts as a vast limestone sponge that drains off water through sinkholes to underground drainage systems. The drainage systems are far too deep to permit the formation of the caved-in natural wells or *cenotes* that dot the northern part of Yucatan. This fact deprived the Peten Maya of both a source of water and the romantic, if quite mistaken, legends of sacrificed virgins. (It would be inelegant beyond words to cast a virgin into a sinkhole.) Instead, water collects where small pockets of clay prevent drainage and form *aguadas,* some of which hold water year round. Since *aguadas* are a small and rather undependable water source, the Maya supplemented them by man-made reservoirs. There are also a number of small lakes scattered across the Peten. The largest of them, Lake Peten Itza, is set, like a jewel in a ring of rain forest, in almost the exact center of the Peten, about 20 miles south of the major Maya site of Tikal. Although lakes must have been locally important as sources of fresh water and fish, they were not numerous enough to have had a major impact on the Maya lifestyle.

Although one could walk for days through the center of the lowlands without crossing anything resembling a stream or river, the borders of the area do have surface drainage. The southern edge of the lowlands is crossed by the Pasion River, which rises as a series of mountain streams in the fastnesses of the Guatemalan highlands. Where the Pasion is joined by the Lacantun River at the southwestern corner of the lowlands it takes a great bend northward to become the mighty Usumacinta River, winding its sinuous course around the Chiapas highlands on the western border of the Maya lowlands to cross the Tabasco coastal plain and empty into the Gulf of Mexico. The Pasion-Usumacinta drainage is lined by a series of fabled ruins, and the river must have been an important route of prehistoric commerce and communication. At the eastern edge of the southern lowlands, several short rivers drain the country of Belize into the Caribbean. Although they must have been of importance to local inhabitants, none of these rivers is part of a major river system.

The climate of the southern lowlands is characterized by a summer rainy season and winter dry season. Rains usually begin in May. The day of the Holy Cross, May 3, is the traditional day on which the first rains are expected. The rainy season follows the typical tropical pattern of clear, sunny mornings giving way to buildups of clouds that bring afternoon and evening thundershowers. Patterns of the storms are localized and hard to predict; natives of the area when asked if it will rain on any particular day will survey the sky knowledgeably and almost invariably reply, "It might."

In this part of Latin America there is a weak tendency toward a split rainy season, with May and June rains followed by a four- to six-week period of lesser rainfall. This midsummer, mini-dry season, called the *canicula* locally, is quite unpredictable. Some years it produces several weeks of clear and beautiful weather; other years it is fervently anticipated and much discussed while the rains continue unabated. In late August the rains begin in earnest, and September and October are among the rainiest months of the year. By late December the dry season has begun and only sporadic showers may be anticipated until the following May.

The amount of rainfall varies from one part of the southern lowlands to another. At Tikal, near the northern edge of the Peten, annual rainfall averages about 50 inches per year. To the south, as one approaches the rain-catching northern slopes of the Guatemalan mountains, rainfall increases until in some of the foothill zones it regularly exceeds 100 inches annually.

Rainfall varies considerably from year to year, but in terms of the vital agrricultural system, there is plenty of latitude for variation. Minor droughts do occur and undoubtedly affect crop yields, but even if the regular planting is lost completely because of failure of the rains to start on time, it is still possible to replant in time for a harvest before the end of the rainy season.

Temperatures in the Peten are not so extreme as one might expect for a tropical rain forest area. Daily maxima are usually between 80 and 90 degrees, and only on rare days in the hottest period at the end of the dry season will the temperature reach 100 degrees. Nighttime temperatures drop into the 70s. Occasional cold spells in the winter may send the thermometer into the 50s, but frost is totally unknown. Humidity, however, is very high, especially during the rainy season, and clothes that are not aired and sunned regularly soon assume a gentle green color from accumulated mold. The humidity can have other disturbing side effects, as, for instance, when one of the archaeologists working at Tikal had a chronic ear problem instantly relieved when a doctor removed several tiny mushrooms that had taken root in his auditory meatus.

Tropical rain forest is, of course, the natural climax vegetation of the southern lowlands (Figure 3). In spite of the fact that rain forest is outside the range of experience of inhabitants of our northern climes, most of us have a distinct image of what it must be and a predisposition to like or dislike it intensely on first encounter. Rain forest differs in several important ways from the temperate forests with which we are familiar. First, the trees do not lose their leaves seasonally, so rain forest is evergreen rather than deciduous like most forests in the United States. Another characteristic of rain forest is the great variety of trees inextricably mixed together. Stands of a single kind of tree, familiar to us in our pine or oak formations, are very rare in rain forest, since conditions favor the juxtaposition of varied

Figure 3

The Rain Forest Floor. *Rain forest vegetation is characterized by a profusion of plant species. (The University Museum, University of Pennsylvania.)*

species and genera. Also, rain forest has a closed canopy, a layer of leafy vegetation so dense that sunlight reaches the ground in very few places. Finally, woody plants dominate the forest completely. Low-lying plants like shrubs, bushes, and ferns are not at all common; the canopy so restricts the passage of sunlight that vegetation has little chance to grow at the level of the forest floor. Consequently, the forest is relatively open and can usually be traversed with little difficulty other than walking around the great buttresslike roots of the taller trees. Travel is quite a different story in areas where the forest has been cut or where a giant tree has fallen, taking with it all the smaller trees in its path and creating a clearing. In these areas, where sunlight can reach the ground, an impenetrable tangle of secondary vegetation soon springs up, which requires all of the cutting and thrashing familiar to devotees of jungle movies.

The most characteristic stands of rain forest occur on higher, well-drained land. Here the forest has at least three stories. The trees of the uppermost story—the tallest species such as mahogany and wild fig, many of which reach 160 to 170 feet in height —protrude above lower stories as emergents. The second story is a dense canopy of somewhat less tall species, still well over 100 feet high. And finally, 30 to 50 feet above the ground, is the lowest story. Parasitic and aerial plants abound; lianas hang in clusters from the lowest tree stories, and wild orchids blossom unnoticed high among the foliage. Although there are some flowering trees like the salmon-colored *amapola*, the forest is generally lacking in color. It is filled with characteristic odors, however—the ever-present greenhouse smell of moist earth and decaying vegetation, the pungent and somewhat unpleasant summer smell of ripe *ramón* nuts, or the incredibly beautiful fragrance of the night-blooming *nopal*.

Lower, less well-drained areas foster variations in vegetation. The damp, but not really swampy, areas of intermediate elevation that we refer to, in a magnificent contradiction in terms, as "high *bajo*" have a less dense canopy, more ground-level plants, and a high frequency of the vicious *escoba* palm, whose trunk is covered with thousands of four-inch spines that await the hand of the unwary traveler who may reach out to it for support. The most swampy areas have still another type of vegetation marked by an abundance of the remarkable logwood tree, whose wood is so dense that it sinks immediately to the bottom in a pool or a pail of water.

Many of the forest tree species are useful to man. The valuable tropical hardwoods, such as mahogany, cedar, or the less-known *sapodilla*, a forest giant that may live to an age of more

than a thousand years, provide superb materials for construction and the manufacture of artifacts. Although most of the
evidence has long since disintegrated in the moist climate, there remain enough hints to indicate that the prehistoric Maya were skilled and enthusiastic wood-workers. Several species of tree provide edible fruits and the *ramón*, or breadnut tree, yields an abundance of hard seed that can be ground into a nutritious flour. The sap of the *sapodilla* yields *chicle*, the base of modern chewing gum, while the gum of the *copal* tree is a fragrant incense that is still widely used by native Indian populations in their religious ceremonies.

The rain forest teems with animal life, but in a quiet and unobtrusive way rather than with the conspicuous majesty of the giant creatures of Old World jungles. American forest mammals are generally wary and difficult to notice. The awesome jaguar, the tapir (like a visitor from the prehistoric past), deer, peccary, and the delicate brocket, looking for all the world like a miniature and badly designed deer, are the major large mammals. Spider monkeys delight in treetop acrobatics and complain vociferously when disturbed by human visitors, while the larger howler monkeys more frequently sit quietly in dour contemplation. Small mammals of kinds such as the tepisquintli, aguti, pisote, and coati, which are familiar only to ardent zoo enthusiasts, are not uncommon. With the exception of a few small species that happily forage on agricultural crops, most of these animals are shy and forest dependent and become increasingly scarce as human populations and cleared land increase. At the time of the dense populations of Late Classic times, meat from a successful hunting expedition was probably a rare delicacy for the Maya.

Birds are considerably more abundant than mammals, and a number of species are edible. The ocellated turkey, which was kept as a captive, the curassow, and the tropical pheasant are still abundant game birds. Parrots and toucans add splashes of color to the forest and supply a noisy commentary upon forest happenings. Although these latter birds could hardly be proclaimed edible even by the least discriminating, their plumage was an indispensable part of pre-Columbian finery and probably provided a major export product of the lowlands. Water birds such as cormorants or the occasional seasonal visitors from the migratory flyways gather at lakes and larger water holes, while myriads of small and, to all but the expert, unnamed species fill the air and trees with song and feather.

But perhaps more than any other living thing, the insects find rain forest a tropical paradise. Hundreds of species of unimaginable shapes and colors whir or buzz or squeal according to their custom, and such unlikely creatures as fluorescent orange centipedes, green and gold horseflies, and shaggy white caterpillers strain the credulity of the careful observer. Many of the insects stand prepared to sting or bite or burrow, but they are more discomforts than dangers for human populations. I have never in the Peten been forced to flee to shelter as I have been by midwestern U.S. mosquitoes.

Amphibians and reptiles also find the Maya lowlands to their liking. Many kinds of toads and frogs are eclipsed in interest by the remarkable *Uo* frog, which for almost the entire year bides his time deep underground, only occasionally grumbling the deep-throated "Woe" for which he is named, to emerge on the wettest day or two of the rainy season for an ecstatic orgy of mating. Snakes are omnipresent and range from the deadly and aggressive fer-de-lance to the gentle and rather friendly Central American boa. Natives of the area regard all snakes with loathing and attack them with a vengeance that would be an inspiration to the buxom lady in the comic strip "B.C." I remember once interrupting one of our workmen, who was stalking a pretty little greenish-blue snake with a large stick, to ask whether the snake was poisonous. He opined that it was a rather small snake and probably harmless, but then noted that "one can never be sure" and proceeded on his quest with great relish.

The southern Maya lowlands are rich in only a few natural resources. Rain forest hardwood, *copal* incense, and the plumage of tropical birds have already been mentioned. Limestone for construction is abundant and readily available. To obtain limestone, it is only necessary to remove a foot or two of topsoil and break through a slightly hardened cap of bedrock to reach inexhaustible supplies of very soft stone that can easily be quarried and shaped even with the simplest kind of tools. The limestone can also be burned to make lime plaster, a technique the Maya handled with skill and ease. Interbedded in the limestone are occasional deposits of chert, a flintlike rock that fractures easily to provide a good material for the manufacture of tools.

Aside from these few items, the natural resources of the southern lowlands are strikingly deficient. Many things that the Maya needed in their way of life were lacking, at least in the central part of the lowlands. Salt, physiologically necessary for the Maya diet, was available only along the coastline of Yucatan and at salt springs at the borders of the Guatemalan highlands. Hard volcanic stone to make the *manos* and *metates*, with which the Maya ground their daily ration of corn, and obsidian, the volcanic glass that provides a cutting edge of unparalleled sharpness, could be procured only from the Maya Mountains or from surrounding highland territories. These items of interest to the everyday housewife, and doubtless a source of vigorous housewifely complaint if they were missing, are, in our new view of the Maya, considered to have been the focus of a vigorous trading network. Materials of value for religious ceremonies also come from distant areas. Shells, coral, and pearls were "musts" as ceremonial offerings and had to be imported. Jade, a symbol of water and life and probably the most valuable of all materials; hematite; and pigments of volcanic origin were also imported to give ceremonies their proper exotic touch. In a resource-deficient area, the Maya must have been forced to considerable efforts in their search for raw materials to make their life what they thought it should be.

2. The Preclassic Background

The Classic period of Maya history is the part between A.D. 250 and A.D. 900. It is traditionally divided into an Early Classic (A.D. 250–600) and a Late Classic (A.D. 600–900). The temporal boundaries of the period are fixed by the fact that this was the time when the Maya left carved inscriptions bearing dates in their highly accurate "long count" system of calendric notation. The Maya calendar was deciphered and inscriptions eagerly recorded in the very early days of Maya studies; thus a large corpus of dated inscriptions had been collected before anyone knew very much about the sites at which the inscriptions occurred. In the absence of other evidence, the tacit assumption was made that all other Maya achievements dated from the same period as the inscriptions. Hence it was concluded that there must have been a six-century period of cultural exuberance and sophistication that might be termed Classic. Since those early days in Maya studies, the accumulation of additional evidence has demonstrated that the Maya achieved a highly complex culture several centuries before the first calendrical carvings. But even though the Classic period no longer has such clean cultural boundaries, it retains its association with calendar dates as a result of habitual usage. Ingeniously, the preceding period, from the first villages to the beginning of the Classic, has been labeled the Preclassic, and the succeeding period, from the Classic to the Spanish Conquest, the Postclassic.

An excursion into Preclassic times is necessary to set the stage for a consideration of Classic culture. Before about 800 B.C., the Maya lowlands may have lain silent and undisturbed by man's busy ways, since no concrete evidence of earlier human occupation has been encountered. Then the first pottery-making, and presumably sedentary and agricultural, populations appeared. Evidence for these first occupants has been recovered from three sites—Altar de Sacrificios and Seibal, both on the Pasion River toward the southern edge of the lowlands, and Barton Ramie, to the east in Belize. At all three sites, soundings below later occupation levels have revealed the early pottery overlying the sterile bedrock. Not much is known about the makers of the pottery; debris is very scattered and there is no evidence of major structures. A scattered occupation by small farming groups is what one could expect to find at this early stage of development, and the archaeological data are clearly compatible with such a reconstruction. It is likely that the first villagers were migrants seeking opportunity in the empty rain forest. Exactly where they came from is still uncertain, but there are plenty of possible sources, since the Maya lowlands was one of the last areas in Mesoamerica to be occupied by farming peoples.

More immigration and population growth followed the first arrivals and by 500 B.C. most of the Maya lowlands seems to have had at least some population. From this point, the Maya were not long in developing features that indicate that their culture was moving in the direction of increased complexity. The best archaeological evidence of this complexity was the early appearance and rapid spread of what was always to be the hallmark of Maya zeal and organization—the temple center. There is every indication that the prehistoric Maya were a genuinely religious people. Their gods meant much to them, and their energy in worship and in providing the trappings for worship was unflagging. More than this, religious participation seems to have been one of the keystones that bound social classes into a cooperative, functioning system and provided pleasure and entertainment through fiestas and pageantry. By the time of Christ, temple centers were commonplace in the Maya lowlands. Detailed information about them is scanty, however, because sacred places were hallowed ground, built upon for generation after generation until almost all early temples were buried under massive Classic construction. Only the largest and best-funded of archaeological projects have the wherewithal to do systematic explorations at the depths required to reach Preclassic remains.

To provide specifics by way of illustration, I must, as I will throughout the book, turn to data from the Tikal Project. Tikal, in the very heart of the Maya lowlands, is perhaps the largest of Maya sites. It consists of acre upon acre of still-magnificent stone buildings juxtaposed with the low mounds that are what remain of the inhabitants' houses. Since 1956, a project from the University Museum, University of Pennsylvania, has been at work in Tikal, and since 1960 I have had the good fortune to participate in the project with colleagues whose skill as archaeologists and whose knowledge of the Maya I greatly respect. Tikal, then, comes easily to my mind—it is the example *par excellence* of Classic Maya achievements, and it is what I know best.

Tikal also provides a forum for the discussion of problems of archaeological method. The very size of the site makes such problems acute and raises a series of methodological questions. How, for instance, can one get an adequate knowledge of a site that has more than 2000 visible structures? To excavate a large temple or palace can take five years of intensive effort; even to dig a group of a dozen housemounds adequately may demand a full season. How can one handle hundreds of large structures and thousands of housemounds? Or, given the Maya custom of continuing to rebuild major structures in a single location, constantly ripping out old buildings and reusing the materials in new ones, how can one find out about earlier periods? Many of the last buildings to be constructed are architectural gems in an excellent state of preservation. Even if cost were not prohibitive (which it is), the destruction of these relatively recent structures could not be justified for a science whose emphasis is upon conservation of ancient remains. These, and scores of other problems, faced us continually at Tikal. We did not solve them all, but we tried, and in the process of trying discovered some things that worked well. We can also, with the inspired light of hindsight, say what we wished we had done and would do if we were starting over again.

From the time of its inception in 1956, one of the chief aims of the Tikal Project was the discovery of the archaeological remains and cultural patterns of the Preclassic Maya. Most earlier archaeological research in the Maya lowlands had been of too small scale to tackle the deeply buried Preclassic levels. Although Preclassic pottery had been encountered at some sites and a few small structures had been excavated, the most promising locations for Preclassic ceremonial precincts, diretly underneath the largest Classic structures, had boggled the budgets of earlier projects. Meanwhile, in other parts of Mesoamerica very large Preclassic centers were known (thanks to prehistoric inhabitants who had been courteous enough toward archaeologists to build Classic centers in new locations, leaving early remains exposed and easy to investigate). A major question remained unresolved: Had the Preclassic Maya been culturally retarded in comparison with their neighbors? Were the simple structures that had been discovered the best the Maya could accomplish before the start of the Classic? If the answer was yes, there was even the possibility that Maya Classic culture was a transplant, imposed on humble local peasants by people from outside.

Most Mayanists reacted uncharitably toward the last suggestion, but the only way to resolve the issue definitively was to excavate in central and very difficult locations at major sites.

At Tikal a logical place to meet the Preclassic problem head on was the North Acropolis, a gigantic man-made platform closing the north side of the Great Plaza. The Acropolis platform stood 40 feet above the plaza floor; symmetrically distributed over its more than 2-acre surface were 11 large temples. Most of the temples on the Acropolis were of Early Classic date—although they had been refurbished and used throughout the Late Classic—so Preclassic structures were likely to be closer to the surface than in areas where there was heavy Late Classic construction. The decision was made to dig a great trench into the North Acropolis, zig-zagging around the Classic temples to avoid unnecessary destruction, and continuing downward, regardless of obstacles, to whatever might be at the bottom (Figure 4).

The trench has now been completed, and the results are even more rewarding than the hopeful estimates made before the project was started. Early Classic platform floors proved to be little more than a thin skin at the surface. Of 33 feet of construction encountered before the bottom of the trench was finally reached, better than 30 feet were pure Preclassic material. Fifteen of the 20 superimposed floors discovered were Preclassic, as were 6 of the 8 reconstructions of the North Terrace, the step between the North Acropolis and Great Plaza. The incredibly detailed record provided by the maze of buildings, modifications, and rebuildings is a resounding demonstration that the Maya achieved the skills and sophistication of a highly advanced culture centuries before the moment that we have assigned as the start of the Classic period.

Only a brief resumé of some of the high points of the Preclassic North Acropolis is possible here (Figure 5). The earliest architecture identified at the bottom of the Acropolis was a small platform built sometime in the third century B.C. and shortly thereafter reconstructed twice with little change. Only the front section of these platforms was preserved; the entire back area had been ripped out during the later construction efforts. The platforms show carefully cut and shaped stones, and red-painted plaster fragments suggest that at least one of the structures was richly decorated. The destruction of these platforms took place about 100 B.C., when an ambitious new and considerably larger platform was built and floored by Floor 15 (the fifteenth floor from the top of the North Acropolis). Several platforms that once stood upon Floor 15 were identified, but later construction had removed all but the lower few inches of their walls so we can say little about them. Within the hearting of Floor 15 was a burial, Burial 164, an adult in a shallow earth-filled pit accompanied by an offering of pottery vessels, a few jade beads, and a spine from the tail of a stingray (an item used by the later Maya for self-sacrificial bloodletting). Although Burial 164 is far from magnificent, the presence of jade and the stingray spine demonstrates that these items were already of ceremonial significance and that the Maya had established the trade networks necessary to import them from distant sources.

Figure 4

Deep Architectural Excavation at Tikal. *Walls of the trench excavated through the North Acropolis at Tikal tower above the workmen cleaning early levels of construction. Several levels of floors are visible in the sides of the trench. (The University Museum, University of Pennsylvania.)*

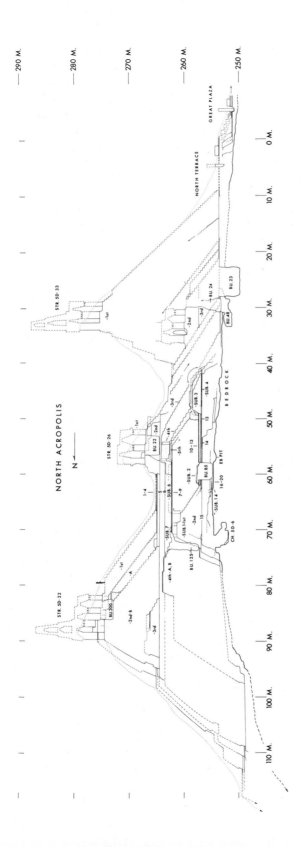

Figure 5

Section of the Tikal North Acropolis. *This illustration shows the layer-cake effect of continuous rebuilding in major architectural precincts. Time after time the Maya rebuilt and enlarged their structures, leaving a buried record of earlier architecture. (The University Museum, University of Pennsylvania.)*

A rapid succession of rebuildings and expansions of the North Acropolis illustrates the growth of economic strength and organization of the Maya. A look at one further construction stage might be informative. This stage, dating to about 50 B.C., was especially well preserved because at a slightly later time the Maya decided to increase the scale of the North Acropolis drastically in a massive enterprise that involved laying 15 feet of fill over the existing floors and buildings. Structures covered by the thick layer of fill are preserved to considerable heights rather than being ripped off almost to floor level, and the block of fill left room for the excavators to open tunnels off the side of the excavation levels to reveal additional features. Tunneling is a risky and time-consuming operation in archaeology, but many times it is the only way that deeply buried features can be followed. The fill used in Tikal structures is fortunately very solid and permits greater safety in tunneling operations than at many sites. The only major collapse of a tunnel system that occurred at Tikal took place in the tunnels around the area now being described. Fortunately, uncovered remains had already been recorded, and the initial trickle of dirt before the collapse provided time for workers to flee.

At least five structural platforms occupied the North Acropolis in 50 B.C. On one of these platforms sat Structure 5D-Sub 1, a truly remarkable example of early Maya architecture. The platform base for Structure 5D-Sub 1 measured 37 by 43 feet and was 14 feet high. It consisted of a complex and striking arrangement in which overlapping planes and angles catch light and create shadow to give the nearly indescribable effect characteristic of the best of Maya architecture. The two-room masonry building that surmounted the platform had unfortunately been cut off at a point just too low to reveal whether it was spanned by the corbeled arch typical of later Maya architecture. The central stairway was flanked by stuccoed and painted masks that seem to have represented jaguar heads, while the upper facade of the building was covered by an intricately carved plaster design painted in cream, black, red, and pink. The complex in its original condition must have been a breathtaking sight, demonstrating the full Preclassic development of Maya architectural and artistic talents.

The same care and artistic taste evident in architecture were lavished upon the dead by the Preclassic Maya. A good example is Burial 166, which was placed in the North Acropolis at about the time of construction of Structure 5D-Sub 1. In a pit dug through the Acropolis floor a tomb was constructed to hold the burial. On the floor of the tomb were placed an adult of undetermined sex (Individual A) and a second individual (B), who was already a disarticulated skeleton. One is tempted to the conclusion that Individual B may have been a relative of lesser status whose remains were honored by being allowed to join the obviously important Individual A in the trip to the afterworld. Tomb offerings included 20 fine pottery vessels, some imported from distant locations, which contained fragmentary remains of perishable materials that may once have been foodstuffs. Skeleton A was bedecked with a necklace of shell and jade beads and a shell pendant carved with the profile of a human head. The plastered walls of the tomb had been painted red and then decorated in black with six human figures, all badly destroyed by the time of discovery but still demonstrating rich costuming and elaborate headdresses. When the tomb was sealed, a small structure was immediately erected over the shaft, probably to serve as a shrine for continued offerings and ceremonies to, or in memory of, the deceased.

Tomb burials of this sort illustrate another important sign of social complexity—the emergence of differences in social rank. Even if religious enterprises—the construction of temples and performance of ceremonies—were regarded with enthusiasm by all the members of Preclassic Maya society, the enterprises are too large to have been accomplished without organization and careful direction. Individuals such as those in Burial 166 must have supplied the direction. In the process, they would have become separated from common people and had access to power and authority and to material possessions.

The excavations in the North Acropolis at Tikal—and excavations conducted since at other sites—remove all doubts about the status of the Preclassic Lowland Maya. They were already well on their way to civilization, and the Classic period was a logical culmination of achievements rather than the transplant of a finished blossom of culture into an unwholesome forest environment.

The important question in the Preclassic–Classic transition is its meaning in terms of the development of Maya civilization. Although we can now dismiss the idea that Maya civilization was an imported product thrust upon a group of naïve villagers, we must still ask whether the beginning of the Classic was associated with sudden and far-reaching changes in Maya society. We do know that most of the architectural elements treated as marks of the Classic were known to the Maya (though not extensively used) considerably earlier. The way in which these elements were combined at the beginning of the Classic, however, is very characteristic and set a typically Maya style that persisted until the sudden collapse of Maya Classic civilization. The process of setting this style might have involved changes in the way Maya society operated. To find out whether it did is a top priority project for future research.

By the Early Classic, the Lowland Maya were civilized. They had reached that status in less than a thousand years since the time at which the first hesitant immigrants had ventured into the green sea of rain forest. One of the major tasks of anthropology is to explain why such events occur; therefore a venture into theory is worthwhile, in an effort to see how well some general ideas about the rise of civilization fit the Maya case.

The first point to note is that the environment of the Maya homeland makes their rise to civilization difficult to understand. Most early civilizations were located in arid lands with major river systems, such as the sun-baked valleys of the Near East, the sparse plain watered by the Huang-ho River in China, or the Peruvian desert coast where rain may occur once a generation. Many theories about the factors causing civilization revolve around the problems of adjusting to these arid environments in which man can create lush oases in the midst of nearly uninhabitable desert. As one might well imagine, such theories sit uneasily upon the Maya.

One such theory is the _irrigation hypothesis_ suggested by the historian Karl Wittfogel and elaborated for Mesoamerica by William T. Sanders. The essence of the hypothesis is that in many of the areas in which early civilizations developed, successful agriculture depended on major irrigation projects. Such public works projects need direction and organization; that is, they must be run by a managerial class. This class has the community's key resources at its fingertips and a built-in mechanism of social control—they can cut off water from a farmer who proves uncooperative. The end result is an Oriental despotism (ancient China served as Wittfogel's original model), an extremely centralized and tightly controlled kind of state organization. However exciting this idea may be in the appropriate environment, it runs aground in the Maya lowlands where irrigation cannot be practiced because of a lack of several necessary topographic and hydrographic features.

I think, however, that a similar but more generalized proposition might be applicable both to the Maya lowlands and to the areas in which irrigation may have played a developmental role. This more general proposal centers upon the efficiency of resource management rather than upon one particular kind of food production system. I would suggest that where maximization of production is necessary or desirable, managed economies—that is, economies directed by a class of agents with political authority—will have a competitive advantage. This hypothesis would clearly apply to irrigation civilizations, where the link between management and productivity has already been stressed. As will be discussed in detail in the following chapter on Maya subsistence, I feel the same statement applies to the Lowland Maya even though the Maya system did not involve the need for the huge labor gangs needed for irrigation projects. Although we must reject an irrigation hypothesis as related to the use of Maya civilization, we are left with a *management hypothesis* that may be applicable.

Another theory about the rise of civilizations is an *environmental circumscription theory* proposed by Robert Carneiro. In its most direct form, this hypothesis applies to areas in which small regions of highly fertile land are surrounded by areas that are of low productivity or totally unexploitable. Once again, arid river valleys in which verdant irrigated lands stop at the desert border are a prime example. Carneiro argues that once populations in such oases have filled the good farming areas, they have nowhere left to go; the resultant population pressure leads to warfare over productive resources, which soon culminates in a stratified society with the victors in the struggle dominating the losers. The application of this theory in the rain forest setting of the Maya is a failure, for farmable lands in the Lowland Maya zone extend almost endlessly. To explain areas where there are no environmental borders to circumscribe population, Carneiro suggests the corollary that in such cases a *social circumscription,* in which a community may be circumscribed by neighboring communities, can create overpopulation, with the same result as that following on environmental circumscription. I find this corollary far from convincing, because it fails to explain why social circumscription occurs in some areas and not in others.

Another environmentally based hypothesis has been suggested by Kent V. Flannery to account for a key civilizational characteristic—*social stratification.* Flannery's suggestion is that in a developing area that has lands of drastically different value for agricultural productivity, the good lands will be occupied first. Then as population expands, lands of lower quality will have to be used. Individuals or groups that in earlier days had gained control over the best lands will have the bulk of the society's resources at their command and will hence be in an excellent position to form an elite and directing class. Like the previous hypothesis, Flannery's suggestion fits best those semiarid areas occupied by most early civilizations. In the Maya rain forest, there do not seem to be nearly so great differences in the pro- ductivity of different sections, and one would expect that the general availability of large quantities of relatively equivalent land would mitigate against the formation of classes by the mechanism noted. It must be admitted, however, that we have very little information on land variation in the Maya lowlands, and to reject Flannery's idea before some good ecological studies have been done is probably premature.

Recently, a theory has been proposed by William L. Rathje to explain the origin of complex societies in environments like that occupied by the Lowland Maya. This theory, which features the _control of trade_ as a major factor in the growth of an elite, directorial class, is centered not so much upon luxury items as upon basic resources—materials needed or greatly desired for daily use by people at all levels of society. Rathje points out that the Maya lowlands are lacking in several kinds of basic resources. Most important among these are salt (a physiological necessity not present in sufficient amounts in the daily food of largely vegetarian people like the Maya), hard stone (which every Maya housewife needed for corn-grinding tools), and obsidian (a black volcanic glass from which the Maya and many other peoples fashioned razor-sharp cutting tools). The closest sources of these materials lie outside, or at the borders, of the Maya lowlands, far distant from the heaviest concentrations of lowland population. Crucial to Rathje's developmental concept is a distinction between the central part of the Maya lowlands —Rathje calls it the _core area_—and the fringes of the lowlands —the _buffer zone_.

In securing basic resources, buffer zone inhabitants have a natural advantage over core area inhabitants. Some resources are within the buffer zone or close enough to it to be reached by short expeditions of small groups of people. For resources that are controlled by groups outside of the lowlands, the buffer zone can offer a series of exotic forest products, transported more easily and cheaply than they can be from the core. One might think that the result would be that the buffer zone inhabi- tants would become rich, while those in the core languished. Just the opposite was apparently the case, however, since the largest, earliest, and most luxurious Maya sites are overwhelm- ingly in the core area.

Rathje has an explanation for this seeming anomaly. He proposes that to settle in the core area at all (and secure the outside resources they felt necessary) centrally located groups must have very rapidly developed the organization necessary to conduct long-distance trade. Core area sites, then, had the jump on buffer zone sites in organization and maintained their edge as both zones developed. In essence, core area groups, for lack of anything else, had to specialize in organization. In addition, since the core area lacked any natural resources that the buffer zone might want, sites there developed artificial resources— especially a ceremonial system and its trappings. Buffer zone sites, since they were participants in the same religious and ideological system, found these ceremonial niceties desirable enough to induce them to tranship outside raw materials to the core. One can almost imagine marketing research and advertising campaigns about the newest ceremony—"30 percent more effective in starting the spring rains." Fragile though it seems in some respects, Rathje's theory fits the facts beautifully. Core sites *were* bigger and earlier and *were* the leaders in Maya ceremonialism.

This review has provided, not one, but several theories that are potentially applicable to the understanding of why the Maya became civilized. This is as I feel it should be, for I must confess a lack of enthusiasm for a suggestion that there is *one* cause of civilization. Civilizations are extremely complex systems consisting of many parts that operate in different, even though eventually interdependent, fashions. Attention to a single aspect is likely to provide one (or several) ideas about interrelationships; attention to other aspects will provide more. An understanding of how things interrelate and react upon one another is an achievable goal that may be a better way to ask questions about the rise of civilization than the pursuit of single causes.

3. The Rise of Maya Classicism

The term "Classic" has a pleasant ring of elegance that conjures up images of art-filled museums or the strains of mighty symphonies. A theme of such intellectual opulence is not inappropriate for the style of Maya life during their own Classic period. The Maya were intellectuals, and one cannot escape the feeling that during the Classic the Maya were at their best—that what gave them their curiously unique appeal reached a peak, hung together for a few brief centuries, and then, like a spider web, disintegrated to shreds and tatters that gave little hint of what once had been.

The appearance of Maya Classic culture was considered at one time to be the result of a sudden burst of achievement; where there had been only the thatched huts of humble farmers, there appeared, as if out of the magician's puff of smoke, the towering temples and talented artists and architects of the Classic. Now that we know more about the dates of things besides carved inscriptions, such magical apparitions are neither realistic nor necessary. By the Late Preclassic, the Maya had already developed, by means of the less striking but more believable process of pulling upward on their own bootstraps for several centuries, the basic framework of a civilization complete with social classes, economic specialization and trade, and large public architecture. The background was there; the tools and institutions were ready; the ideas of rulers and inequality in possessions were already ingrained in the Maya view of how life should be. The Classic brilliance of the Maya was a logical next step. It was, in a sense, predetermined by the paths that development had already taken.

The present realization that a gradual local development preceded the Maya Classic does away with another myth of former years—that Maya civilization may have been a transplant brought by immigrants from some other area. Instead, it is clearly a local product—one that fits the unique circumstances of the rain forest environment and expresses the world view and cosmology of people with deep roots in the area. By no means, however, does this mean that Maya civilization developed in total isolation. Many important ideas were borrowed from elsewhere. Polychrome pottery and the calendar, for instance, seem to have originated outside of the Maya lowlands. There may even have been some migrants into the area who added their ideas and innovations to the developing mixture. What counts, however, is that the form of Maya Classic civilization had a unique stamp. The expression of institutions and ideas, even though they changed through time, remained indelibly Maya—as characteristic of their particular setting as the scent of rain forest or the hook-nosed profile of the Maya priest.

Continuing for the moment an emphasis on the uniqueness of Maya Classic civilization, we must consider some of the features that are most distinctive of Maya lowland sites. If there is one thing that more than anything else is the hallmark of the Maya Classic, it is the carved portraits of sumptuously garbed Maya leaders accompanied by hieroglyphic inscriptions that include dates in the Maya calendar. Usually occurring on the life-sized stone slabs known as *stelae* (Figure 6), such carvings also occur on architectural elements and sometimes on smaller portable objects fashioned from bone or precious stone.

The appearance of hieroglyphic inscriptions has long been considered a useful marker for the beginning of the Maya Classic period. Therefore the search for the earliest carving securely dated by a Maya calendar date has proved an exciting pastime for archaeologists. The story goes back to a day in 1864 when a flash of green in a shovel of mud caught the attention of a crew of canal diggers near Puerto Barrios, Guatemala. The green object proved to be a carved jade pendant, which eventually found a home in the Leyden Rijksmuseum in the Netherlands and became known as the Leyden Plate (Figure 7). On one surface an aloof Maya lord, burdened by a costume and headdress bristling with human and deity masks, stands above a prone, bound captive. Striking though the figure is, it can be matched by scores of similar representations from Maya Classic art; the real fascination of the Leyden Plate is on the obverse where a series of elegant glyphs proclaim the Maya date 8.14.3.1.2., which has been translated as September 15, A.D. 320. In the spate of decipherment that followed cracking of the Maya calendric system in the early 1900s, the Leyden Plate was the earliest date recorded in the Maya Classic system. It also became apparent that the pendant was probably not carved anywhere near the area in which it was discovered, since Puerto Barrios is in a border area of the Maya region, and the style of the plate is very similar to representations at Tikal near the center of the Maya homeland.

The claim of the central Peten to be the homeland of the Maya inscription style was strengthened in 1916 when Sylvanus G. Morley, exploring the newly discovered ruins of Uaxactun,

Figure 6

Stela 1, Ixkun. *Many Maya stelae record events in the lives of famous priest-kings. Here, two priests or leaders meet on a long-forgotten errand. (The Peabody Museum, Harvard University.)*

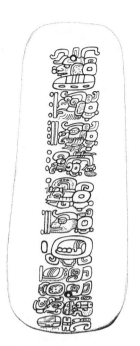

Figure 7

The Leyden Plate. *Carved in* A.D. *320, the Leyden Plate
represents both a fine example of early Maya carving and
one of the earliest dates recorded in the Maya calendrical
system. The common theme of a Maya lord standing
above a bound captive was already established, even
though the date falls very early in the Early Classic
period. (The University Museum, University of Pennsylvania.)*

encountered Uaxactun Stela 9, a badly eroded slab on which
could be faintly discerned a single standing figure and a lengthy
inscription including a date that translates to April 9, A.D. 328,
only seven years and a few months after the day commemorated
on the Leyden Plate. So the situation remained through long
years in which the numbers of newly reported inscriptions
steadily declined as explorers found it more and more difficult
to find unvisited sites with new stelae and inscriptions. It seemed
a near certainty that the claim for earliest inscribed Maya date
would continue to rest with the Leyden Plate.

Then one spring day in 1960, a workman at Tikal noticed
a piece of carved stone barely projecting above the ground in

a little-traveled area of the site. Excavation revealed the stone to be the corner of a stela, which when cleared proved to have a figure decorated with masks of very early style on the up-turned face. The stela, numbered as Tikal Stela 29, was left partially uncovered for several weeks to allow time for the surrounding earth to dry and to allow the staff to attend to other pressing duties. Almost as a spare-time enterprise, Field Director Edwin Shook returned one day to turn the heavy stela and inspect what preliminary groping under the monument had suggested was a smooth stone back. As the encrusted dirt was flaked away, there appeared a simple calendrical inscription —8.12.14.8.15, July 6, A.D. 292—a date 28 years earlier than that of the Leyden Plate. The earliest known Maya inscription was now where it should be, in the very heart of the Maya lowlands in the area where Classic monuments were presumed to have first been erected.

From the date on which Tikal Stela 29 was dedicated, the custom of erecting dated stelae spready slowly at first and affected only sites at the very heart of the Maya lowlands. During Baktun 8, the major Maya time period ending in A.D. 435, stelae were erected only at Tikal, Uaxactun (the major site closest to Tikal), Balakbal (a medium-sized site 35 miles north of Uaxactun), and Uolantun (a tiny site only 5 miles from Tikal).

With the opening of Maya Baktun 9, an explosive spread of the stela cult began. In the first quarter of Baktun 9—A.D. 435–534 in our calendar—ten new centers, scattered to the four corners of the Maya lowlands, adopted the practice of erecting dated monuments. Copan, far to the southeast at the very edge of the lowlands, was represented. So was Tonina—not even in the lowlands, but in an outlying lowland-influenced area on the arid Chiapas plateau. The Pasion River area was included with the erection of a stela at Altar de Sacrificios in A.D. 425, while Piedras Negras and Yaxchilan stelae marked the spread of inscriptions to the western border of the lowlands along the Usumacinta River. At 475, the dedication of a stela at Oxkintok in the thorn forest of northern Yucatan marked the spread of the stela cult almost to the tip of the Yucatan Peninsula. During the last century of the Early Classic period (A.D. 500–600), the stela cult continued to spread, as an additional ten ceremonial centers were added to the list of sites that formally commemorated the key dates of Maya calendric periods. The idea of dated monuments was clearly a huge success.

The attention given to stone carving in the preceding paragraphs may seem to give undue emphasis to Maya art. But the custom of erecting stela was far more than an aesthetic exercise. It was symbolic to the Maya in the same way it has since become symbolic to the archaeologist—as a visible representation of sharing in a set of values and practices of great importance to the way Maya society was organized. That stelae had religious significance is obvious. They were usually placed in front of temples and were associated with caches of valuable objects of symbolic significance. Even today the Maya inhabitants of Guatemala visit famous stelae to burn incense and make offerings to gods whose ancient names they have long since forgotten. The presence of stelae at a Maya site implies that leaders of the site had access to the esoteric and perhaps magical knowledge of priests, scribes, and astronomers.

But stelae are representative of political power and status as well. The individuals portrayed were real and were clearly of immense importance in their time. Specialists can now read enough Maya hieroglyphs to recognize the names of some of the rulers—exotic appellations like Shield Jaguar, Bat Sky, or Jeweled Skull—and to know that the inscriptions celebrate their accomplishments. Sites with stelae participated in high-level power politics and were communities to be dealt with in the games that nations play for power, prestige, and economic gain.

But, of course, additional characteristics mark the Classic period. During this time Maya architectural style also came into full flower. The most distinctive Maya architectural form was the complex consisting of a towering pyramid surmounted by a temple (Figure 8), all constructed from carefully cut stone blocks and covered with dazzling white or gaudily painted plaster. The pyramidal bases for temples were stepped, made of successively smaller units piled one on the other. The body of each step was tapered and corners were frequently inset to create the effect of a single unbroken unit that contrasts with the box-upon-box appearance that characterizes the stepped pyramids of central Mexico (Figure 9). Precipitous stairways sweep up the front of Maya pyramids at unbelievably steep angles. Uncomfortably high steps with treads so narrow that they can accommodate only the toe and ball of the foot makes the steepness possible. The result is perilous, and a misstep on a Maya stairway can be rewarded with an uninterrupted plunge to the plaza floor below.

Surmounting the pyramid is a low platform on which stands the temple. The effect of the vertical boxlike construction of the temple walls is mitigated by a slanting, overhanging molding. Above the temple roof, the complex again reaches skyward with a towering roof comb that overshadows the temple building itself in magnificence. The roof comb, purely decorative in its function, was usually covered with richly sculptured designs in plaster, which are now, unfortunately, almost always too badly preserved to interpret. The pyramid-temple complex forces an impression of soaring height upon the observer. The eye is drawn ever upward to the temple and its roof comb and thence to the sky. The interplay of light and shadow created by the angles and overhangs typical of Maya architecture softens potential starkness and prevents the overdazzling effect that a massive white surface can have in tropical sunlight. The impact in moonlight even surpasses that of day, and it is not

Figure 8

Temple 1, Tikal. *The temple, set on top of a towering pyramidal substructure, is the most characteristic of Classic Maya architectural forms. The inset corners, steep stairway, and roof comb reaching skyward above the temple all stress the verticality of the composition. (The University Museum, University of Pennsylvania.)*

Figure 9

Pyramids at Teotihuacan. *This row of pyramids from the Classic central Mexican site of Teotihuacan demonstrates the differences between Central Mexican and Mayan architecture. The focus here is on horizontal units, piled one on top of the other like a series of boxes.* (Copyright © 1973 by René Millon. All rights reserved.)

difficult even now to imagine hushed ceremonies in the dead of night. Acoustic effects are startling—a softly spoken word from the doorway of Temple 1 at Tikal can be easily distinguished throughout the Great Plaza. Whether the sound-chamber effect is accidental or the Maya included acoustical engineering among their accomplishments, we can be certain that the possibilities did not pass unappreciated during ceremonies.

The interior of Maya temples is disappointing by comparison. Narrow, passagelike rooms offer little space for movement and are made oppressive by the contrast between the bulky masonry and the woefully small open spaces. The cramped rooms of Maya masonry are a direct result of limitations in construction techniques. To span open spaces the Maya used the corbeled arch constructed from stacks of slabs each of which projects slightly beyond the slab beneath. Unlike the true arch, which distributes stress mechanically by means of a capstone, the corbeled arch depends upon the use of brute force—enough weight piled upon the nonprojecting part of each slab so that it cannot topple inward. The principle is very limiting. Only small spaces can be spanned; ceiling heights become inordinately high, and supporting walls must be immense. It seems not unlikely that more than a few Maya architects lost face (and

perhaps their lives) because of unwary exercises that over-
stretched the inherent limitations of the corbeled arch.

In addition to temples, the Maya built another class of structures usually referred to as "palaces." These are lower structures
(not built on pyramids) that typically consist of long series of
rooms frequently connected by interior doorways to form multi-
roomed suites. Despite the regal elegance suggested by calling
such structures palaces, nobody is completely certain about
their function, a matter to be discussed later.

Buildings of both temple and palace types are known from
Preclassic levels of Maya lowland sites, but the custom of continually destroying ancient structures and burying their remains
under enlarged later construction means it it has been impossible
to examine them in much detail. A burst of building, especially
of temples, during the Early Classic has provided more abundant
evidence, particularly since a fairly large number of Early
Classic structures remained in use and consequently were not
covered by later structures, until sites were abandoned. The
primary emphasis in Early Classic construction was on religious
structures, and Early Classic investment of labor and materials
was weighted heavily toward ceremonialism.

It will be instructive to consider what a major Maya site such
as Tikal would have been like during the Early Classic period.
Tikal at that time had a quite different aspect than it was to
have in its Late Classic heyday. The dominant feature of the
site in the Early Classic must have been the North Acropolis,
an immense man-made platform crowned by temples. But what
was to become the Great Plaza in the Late Classic was still not
defined by structures. Temples 1 and 2, which later closed the
east and west ends of the Plaza, were not yet built, and the
Central Acropolis at the south edge of the plaza was far less
imposing than it was in its final form. Instead, a paved plaza
several times the length of the final Great Plaza probably gave
a spacious view to the left and right of the North Acropolis
temples.

To the east, about 200 yards away, an enormous mound of
earth exists today—the largest single construction unit at Tikal,
if it was completely man made. Today nothing remains on its
surface except accumulated forest debris—no platforms or
temples, not even much sign of cut stone. For a long time we
called this vast formless mound the Unfinished Acropolis on the
hunch that the Maya were in the process of building their
most imposing complex of all when they were struck down
by the collapse that decimated them about A.D. 900. One day,
in hopes of getting some good samples of artifacts, I began a

test pit on the very top of our Unfinished Acropolis. Only a few meters below the surface the workmen's picks rang against stone, and walls constructed of shaped blocks began to appear. Most surprising, the pottery in the dirt covering the walls was all of Early Classic types, indicating that the structure had been buried at some time before A.D. 600. We dug no further. Forty feet of what might have been solid construction lay beneath us, and the 800 square yards of the platform top dwarfed the tiny test pit. Time and funds to investigate what lay below were not available, and the mystery awaits another project—although an expedition large enough to handle a job of this sort is hard to envision. I now feel that the great platform is all that remains of another acropolis—not one started late in the history of the site and abandoned before it was finished, but one in operation until Early Classic times, after which it fell into disuse and was perhaps robbed of stones to use in Late Classic building efforts.

To the south of the North Acropolis, about 250 yards away, lies another enigmatic mound called the South Acropolis. The South Acropolis is another 100-yard-square platform, supporting a beautiful group of four Late Classic palaces surrounding a small temple. But these Late Classic structures rest on a floor 40 feet above the surrounding ground level, and the accumulated construction must hide magnificent earlier buildings. If a set of temples surmounted the South Acropolis in Early Classic times, three great acropoli may then have faced each other across acres of plaza interrupted only by a scatter of smaller buildings, making quite a different site concept from the denser pattern of Late Classic times.

The overall distribution of population at Tikal during Early Classic times was more sparse than it was later to become. The tiny clusters of houses that sprang up on every hand during the Late Classic population boom had not yet appeared, and residences were much more scattered. The Early Classic site consisted of a central area largely occupied by stately temple complexes with here and there a few palace groups to serve as administrative centers and residences for the elite class. In outlying regions, neighborhood temples and shrines were built at a few locations, and here and there were the thatched huts of lower-class inhabitants. But the total population may not have been more than a few thousand; many of the lower-class population must have lived in the rural hinterlands near their fields. On feast days the center would have teemed with visiting peasants come to witness the ceremonies and bargain for the craft products made by the townsfolk. But this Early Classic center would have been less a city than its Late Classic counter-part and more like a "vacant ceremonial center"—an imposing focus for ceremonialism, but one with a relatively small corps of permanent residents.

Hieroglyphic inscriptions, which are quite scarce for the Early Classic, do not supply the kinds of historical information available for the Late Classic. Consequently ideas about political systems remain largely guesswork. It is not unlikely that the large centers were independent units—each politically autonomous, although perhaps bound together in complex alliances and confederations. To judge by the dominance of temples among Early Classic structures, religious leaders must have had great influence. Perhaps, in fact, religious authority may have been the source from which paramount rulers in the society were drawn. William L. Rathje has argued, from the distribution of burial goods, that Early Classic Maya society remained relatively fluid, so that people could advance their social positions on the basis of their own talents and efforts. For a still-youthful, expanding society that had not yet begun to strain the limits of its resources, such mobility would not be unexpected.

The major power that the Early Classic Maya had to face outside of the lowlands centered at Teotihuacan, a fabulous city of 100,000 inhabitants located a few miles south of modern Mexico City. Although Teotihuacan itself is 600 miles from Maya territory, a vast domain under the influence of the site extended all the way to the borders of the Maya lowlands. In the Highland Maya area, the site of Kaminaljuyu, a scant 100 miles from the lowland zone, copied Teotihuacan so faithfully in its architecture that archaeologists have concluded that it must have been captured and occupied by the Mexicans. That the Lowland Maya interacted with the forces of Teotihuacan is obvious from many kinds of evidence. Teotihuacan-style pottery was faithfully imitated by Maya craftsmen and was very popular throughout the lowlands. The principal god of Teotihuacan, Tlaloc, a goggle-eyed deity associated with the life-giving rains, was occasionally commemorated by the Maya.

Perhaps the most striking evidence of Teotihuacan contact occurs on Stela 31 from Tikal, dated at A.D. 445. On the front of the stela is a completely traditional Maya figure almost hidden amidst the lavish embellishments of his costume. On one side of the stela, however, is a quite different figure (Figure 10), far less elaborately garbed, although he wears a flowing head-dress of feathers. This second figure is distinctly non-Maya. His face lacks the characteristic hooked-nose Maya profile. He carries over his left arm a shield (or perhaps a textile hanging)

1

2

3

Figure 10

Mexican on Stela 31, Tikal. *This dignitary, depicted on one side of Stela 31 at Tikal, seems to be a visitor from Teotihuacan in Mexico. The shield or textile hanging over his left arm bears the image of the goggle-eyed Mexican deity, Tlaloc, while in his right hand he bears a spear thrower, a weapon never used by the Classic Maya. His profile also lacks the hooked nose so characteristic of Maya personages. (The University Museum, University of Pennsylvania.)*

bearing the visage of the Mexican god Tlaloc, while in the other hand he carries a spear-thrower—a typical Teotihuacan weapon not used by the Maya. There seems little doubt that a visitor from Teotihuacan was important enough to have his portrait carved in the company of a Maya leader. What was the meaning of this unique meeting that took place almost 1500 years ago? Several people have interpreted the glyphs on the stela as evidence of political interference from Teotihuacan in the reign of

Tikal. This seems highly unlikely to me, given the lack of any stronger evidence of Teotihuacan military power in the Maya lowlands. I prefer the interpretation that Stela 31 may commemorate the arrangement of an alliance or economic agreement between the lords of Tikal and emissaries from Teotihuacan, by which the two powers attempted to cement commercial agreements to their mutual advantage and profit. The Lowland Maya would certainly have controlled desirable resources absent in the mountain homelands of the *Teotihuacanos*, who, in return, would have been a prime source of the highland products so important to the Maya. Teotihuacan was clearly a power that controlled immense commercial resources—the vast area under its sway may, in fact, have been more of a trade state than a political empire. Recent history not to the contrary, simple good sense would seem to dictate that the leaders of Teotihuacan would have been better off making peaceful trade agreements with the Lowland Maya then embarking upon tactically disadvantageous jungle warfare in an area far from their homeland.

The entire tenor of the Early Classic period suggests cosmopolitan openness. It is obvious that the Maya were thoroughly familiar with important centers outside their own area, and one can easily imagine the same interest and fascination with Teotihuacan styles and customs that Americans have (and had even more strongly a generation or two ago) in the fashion and culture centers of Europe. The widespread contacts of the Maya elite class are demonstrated by the goods found in rich tomb burials. Brightly painted pots decorated in Teotihuacan style mingle with vessels from the Pacific coast of Guatemala and others from a variety of sources within the lowlands. The repetition of the same designs on vessels from different sources suggest that the pottery may have been specifically dedicated to individual rulers. Shell from every coastline in Mesoamerica and jade and obsidian from a series of highland sources demonstrate the breadth of trade contacts. Workmanship on all these items is lavish, and thousands of man-hours of the labor of highly trained artisans is represented in each rich burial.

One gains the distinct impression, then, that the Early Classic period was a time of nearly unqualified success for Maya lowland civilization. The Maya system was functioning smoothly and effectively and still had room for expansion. The results seem to have been growth, continually increasing prosperity, and open and generally peaceful communication both within the lowlands and with peoples outside of the rain forest area.

4. The Subsistence System

Civilizations must eat, so a prerequisite for the emergence of civilization is a subsistence (food-producing) system that will reliably provide plentiful quantities of foodstuffs. Whether the Maya enjoyed an adequate subsistence system is a topic that has been debated endlessly since it was first realized that the Maya built a civilization in their unlikely forested homeland. The problem revolves around the potential productivity of the tropical rain forest. Rain forest agriculture can easily support small scattered populations, but such populations are losers in the quest for greater societal complexity. If population increases in a rain forest area, the environmental base, like a size 9 dress on a size 14 lady, is obviously and glaringly inadequate.

In a sense, Maya civilization was, for a long time, a theoretical embarrassment, for it seemed to defy principles of ecological possibility. The problem now seems at the threshold of a solution—a solution that rests not on rejecting ecological principles, but on reinterpreting the way in which the Maya made a living.

The best starting point in a consideration of Lowland Maya agriculture is the system used by Maya farmers of today. This system, the bane of agricultural production experts and the delight of conservative peasant farmers, is called by the general term slash-and-burn agriculture or, more specifically in Mesoamerica, the _milpa_ system. It is a cycle that consists of cutting vegetation in either the forest or an old abandoned field, burning the dried debris, planting crops for a year or two, and then abandoning the plot for some years to allow natural vegetation to return.

The operation of cutting vegetation is a laborious and time-consuming dry-season project. The important tool in the operation as it is practiced today is the _machete,_ the ever-present and ever-faithful companion of the Mesoamerican peasant. In prehistoric times when metal tools were a thing of the still-unknown future, stone axes must have been used, probably at the cost of considerably greater labor.

In the clearing process, large trees are killed by removing a ring of bark from around the trunk and leaving them standing to meet their inevitable fate. The debris from cutting is allowed to dry in the fields—a not very rapid process with humidity consistently above 50 percent—until just before the start of summer rains, when it is burned (Figure 11). Burning is a worry-provoking process in which good timing is essential. The vegetation must be dry enough to burn well, but a farmer who waits too long runs the risk of being caught by an early start of the rainy season and left with an embarrassing field of trash rather than a cornfield. Most farmers choose a clear and not-too-windy day in late April for burning; a plane flight over a heavily farmed area at that time of year shows a gentle bluish-white haze punctuated here and there by tiny scarlet circles of flame. Maya farmers consider burning to be a very essential step—they say it makes the soil sweat, providing proper nourishment for the germinating seeds. They may be right, even though they have misidentified the essential ingredient, since some

Figure 11

Burning *Milpa. A good burn of cut vegetation is essential in* milpa *agriculture. (Courtesy Richard E. W. Adams.)*

agronomists feel that the ashes provide key nutritive elements that would not be available without burning. Planting is the next step. This is still done with a venerable tool, the sharp-pointed digging stick, the origins of which probably go back as far as farming itself. Small holes are made in the soil every pace or two, grains of corn dropped in, and the hole covered with a quick shuffle of the foot. Rather than the stately, dance-like progress of the wheat sower, the *milpero* has an ungainly gait like an inch-worm moving spasmodically to his unknown goal. Since the planting process involves neither plowing nor turning the soil except for the tiny planting holes, tree trunks or stoney outcrops are not a problem (Figure 12). Traversing a *milpa*, particularly one that has been cut from virgin forest, can demand commandolike diligence in scrambling over partly burned logs and large rocks.

If planting has been well timed, the sprouting corn is watered by the first rains and the growing season is underway. A corn-

Figure 12

Milpa Ready for Planting. *Debris remaining from the burning process is no obstacle to planting done by means of a digging stick and hand sowing. This picture shows a modern Yucatecan* milpa *ready for planting. (Courtesy Richard E. W. Adams.)*

field demands relatively little labor during the growing season. A light weeding or two is useful, and measures must be taken to decrease loss of plants to animal and insect predators, but this still leaves ample time in the schedule for nonfarming activities. Harvest, which usually takes place in October or November, involves a period of back-breaking labor, but the rewards of a full storage shed make it a time of happiness followed by celebration.

Planting the same field is easier the second year, for only the off-season growth of vegetation needs to be cleared. But the corn grows noticeably less well, and yields may be no more than an expected, but still disappointing, 70 percent of the first season's harvest. If the field is planted a third time, the process of diminishing returns continues, and stubborn clumps of grass begin to compete with the growing crops. Not surprisingly, few farmers find it worth the effort to make three successive plantings in the same field. The rapid slump in production from one crop year to the next is the key problem in lowland *milpa* agriculture. Several different reasons have been proposed to account for it, and it is likely that all are involved in part. One reason is a loss of soil fertility. Tropical soils that have been denuded of natural vegetation and exposed to high rainfall and temperatures lose key nutritive elements very rapidly. Another problem with continued cropping in the same field is grass invasion, which is very difficult to combat with hand methods and native tools. If grass invasion reaches the point at which a continuous sod has formed, further farming is next to impossible because sod cannot be broken with simple digging sticks. Finally, it has recently been suggested that continued cropping leads to a buildup of insects that prey upon food plants. In the virgin forest there is a great variety of insects, only a few of which are damaging to crops. As a field continues to be used, the crop predators are favored and increase rapidly. In effect, the farmer is raising insect pests as well as corn.

Acting on the principle that the best defense against insurmountable problems is to bail out, the Maya farmer abandons a field after two years of planting. Exuberant secondary vegetation takes over, and in a few years natural processes rebuild the ability of the land to produce high yields when it is farmed once again. The period of fallow allowed before clearing a field varies considerably among farmers in lowland Mesoamerica, but it seems never to be less than three years, and six to eight years is about average. As a result of the long fallow period, each farming family must have a considerable amount of land at its disposal, since for each plot actually under cultivation three or four plots will be in fallow.

The exigencies of lowland slash-and-burn farming have strong implications for the size and distribution of population. First, population density must be low because each family needs so much land to operate its farming cycle. Among modern *milpa* farmers in lowland Mesoamerica, densities range between 25 and 100 persons per square mile. A second important feature is that it is extremely difficult to support dense population aggregates such as large towns or cities. Even assuming indefatigable energy, there is a limit to how far a farmer can walk and still have time left for farming once he reaches his fields. Today this limit seems to be about five miles, and since it seems safe to consider the number of hours in the day and the length of legs as fairly constant through time, the limit can be accepted for prehistoric periods as well. A single community, then, can accommodate only as many farmers as can find land within a five-mile radius. Any additional people who live there must be nonfarmers and must be supported from the surplus production of the agricultural population. It is obvious that the land-wasteful *milpa* system, which has a relatively low margin of surplus production, will act against the formation of large communities.

The foregoing description is based upon ethnographic evidence. It is the way lowland rain forest agriculture operates today, and it has long been assumed by archaeologists that the prehistoric Maya operated in exactly the same fashion. *If the milpa* system is the most productive subsistence system possible in the Maya lowlands, Maya civilization faced severe limitations on population density, necessitating scattered settlement and limited community size. But does this picture fit the archaeological facts? In a general sense, it does. Maya archaeological sites, although they show impressive clusters of civic architecture, do not give evidence of the crowding of people into limited areas that is the mark of true cities. Furthermore, prehistoric Maya residential sites are scattered quite evenly through the rural hinterlands between ceremonial centers.

As more detailed figures for population accumulate through archaeological research, however, flaws appear in the fit with the predicted pattern. Most modern archaeological projects are concerned with prehistoric demography and make an effort to estimate population size by counting samples of housemounds. Such estimates are fraught with serious methodological problems, but for the moment we will accept them at face value. There are population estimates for three sites in the Maya lowlands. At Tikal the figures suggest a density of 1600 per square mile; at Dos Aguadas, a smaller site in the central Peten, the counts provide an estimate of 575 per square mile; and

Barton Ramie, toward the eastern edge of the lowlands, shows a density of 1400 per square mile. Compared with modern densities of 25 to 100 people per square mile, it is clear the prehistoric figures are far too high for *milpa* farmers.

The same sort of problem exists concerning the size of Maya ceremonial centers. Tikal, probably the largest of the centers and one of the most thoroughly investigated, shows enough house mounds in the six square miles surrounding the site center to accommodate 11,000 inhabitants. Even this estimate makes no allowance for upper-class residents who may have lived in the large stone structures scattered throughout the site —a group that might well add several thousand more inhabitants. Tikal was by no means a vast city—Teotihuacan in the valley of Mexico probably had nearly ten times as many people—but neither was Tikal a vacant town, dusty and deserted except at the time of ceremonies. Certainly a population in excess of 10,000 in a single location would strain the expected support capacities of a *milpa* system of agriculture.

Now that the challenge to theoretical *milpa* support capacities posed by estimates of prehistoric Maya population has been broached, we must return to the question of whether such population estimates are valid. This is a highly debatable question. To explore it means a venture into the glorious and confusing detail involved in moving from a raw set of observable data to the kinds of conclusions that the archaeologist hopes are inherent in the data.

The first problem in producing a figure for the size of a prehistoric population is to locate the living units, which for any food-producing population means finding house sites. If the prehistoric population built houses of imperishable materials such as stone or adobe, this problem may not be severe. Most Maya houses were probably pole and thatch structures (Figure 13) which rapidly turn back to jungle dust, but, to the archaeologists' good fortune, these houses were built on low stone-walled platforms. The platforms *do* get preserved as low mounds that can still be observed and mapped by an eye that pays close attention to surface contours. At Tikal we did enough excavating of small mounds and of areas where no mounds were visible on the surface to convince us that the count of mounds is within 10 percent of the number of platforms that actually existed at the site, a quite acceptable error factor.

Once satisfied of the accuracy of a count of platforms, the archaeologist must either make an assumption about, or devise a test to determine, what percentage of the platforms had been the bases for residential structures rather than serving some other function. At Tikal, a project under the direction of William Haviland was undertaken to excavate a sample of more than 200 small platform mounds. The excavations showed that a great majority of the platforms were very similar in basic design and had associated refuse deposits containing implements that would have been useful in domestic routines. The remaining 16 percent showed unusual design features and/or rubbish that suggested that they had been of different use. Haviland moved then to the assumption that all of the 84 percent of similar platforms had served as foundations for houses. It is not very difficult to think of reasons that would make the assumption incorrect, but compared to some of the assumptions that must be made further on, it is a pillar of strength.

At this point, the investigator has a count of the number of

Figure 13

Maya Pole and Thatch Houses. *Houses such as these, constructed by modern Maya in the highlands of Chiapas, Mexico, are unchanged in fundamental features from those built by the Classic Maya. Made entirely of perishable materials, such houses would leave almost no achaeological evidence except for the fact that they are almost always built on top of small earth platforms. (Arizona State Museum, University of Arizona, William Holland Collection.)*

house platforms and at least some idea of the likely margin of error in his count. But if, as at most Maya sites, the house platforms represent a period spanning many centuries, a population estimate for any particular point in time is still impossible, since none of the evidence so far collected tells *when* any particular house was occupied. The solution to this problem lies in gathering ceramic samples from mounds to compare with a known and dated ceramic sequence. Although in many areas of the world enough pottery can easily be gathered from the surface of structures to provide a date, conditions in rain forest defy surface collecting because accumulated vegetation debris envelops everything to a depth of several inches. In a case of this sort, excavation is the only way to get a ceramic sample. At a large site, excavation of all structures is clearly impossible; therefore some sort of sampling procedure is necessary. At Tikal, we sampled about 10 percent of the more than 1800 small mounds in the central area and 33 percent, chosen by appropriate statistical techniques, in outlying areas of the site. Both results indicated that better than 80 percent of the excavated structures were house platforms occupied during the last half of the Late Classic period, a percentage we feel relatively secure in extending to unexcavated mounds.

At this point in the Tikal excavations, we could say with some security that about 80 percent of the 1800 small mounds at Tikal were the remains of houses occupied during the Imix period, our name for the part of the Late Classic dating from A.D. 700 to 830. Does this mean, however, that all of the houses were lived in during the entire period? Sadly, it does not. The Imix period lasted about 130 years, and the ceramic evidence upon which dates are based is not precise enough to indicate whether particular samples represent the whole period or a part thereof. A pole and thatch house, such as those that must have occupied Tikal house platforms, will survive the rigors of rain forest climate for only about 25 years. We need to decide at this point what the Maya did when their houses began to disintegrate from age. Would they have abandoned house and platform both and started from scratch at a new location? Or would they have saved the effort of building a new platform and simply repaired an old house or built a new one on the same platform? The answer to these questions has a drastic effect on population estimates. If a new platform was built each time a house needed refurbishing, five housemounds dated to a 130-year period like Imix would not indicate five prehistoric families, but would simply be the residue of a single family that changed location each generation.

At Tikal, careful digging has provided some evidence that bears on the problem. Most house platforms that have been
completely excavated show signs of resurfacing, remodeling, and additions. Such efforts would hardly have been necessary if the platforms were used for only 25 years for the original houses for which they were designed. Moreover, if the ceramic evidence is based upon large and carefully excavated samples, it *is* possible to subdivide Imix ceramics. In the few cases where the ceramics were good enough for such exacting estimates, rubbish associated with individual mounds frequently suggests fairly long periods of occupation. Finally, the principle of least effort makes it seem unlikely that the Maya would have been prone to abandon perfectly good platforms and invest the considerable amount of time necessary to build new ones, just because the houses on top of the platforms were getting rickety. Putting these minor clues together, we have chosen to estimate that all Tikal housemounds with Imix pottery were occupied at the same time. The essential point to note, however, is how far out on a limb we are with this conclusion. Evidence at this point in the process of moving to a population estimate is far less secure than evidence used at the points where earlier conclusions had to be reached. Yet we must move ahead or simply give up any hopes of reaching the desired goal of estimating population.

One final step must be taken before coming up with a population estimate. We now have an estimate of how many houses were occupied at a particular point in time. To get a figure for population, we must know how many people lived in an average house. First, it should be noted that Maya house platforms are small and would have provided room for no more than the single-family, one-room houses characteristic of the Maya lowlands today. To say that number of occupied platforms equals number of single families seems safe enough. It is traditional in Maya archaeology to use a figure of five members as the average size of a family. This figure is based upon censuses taken of Indian communities in Mexico not long after the Spanish Conquest. But if one looks at data from around the world, the size of average families can vary considerably from one culture to another, depending on birth and death ratios, family structure (for example, do elderly parents live with children), marriage patterns (for example, are there large numbers of unmarried adults), and other factors. One would hope that sixteenth-century Indian families from Mexico would be a good measure for the Classic Maya, but it is obvious that we cannot be sure. The final step in a population estimate, then, involves one more operation in which reliability is distinctly dubious.

This lengthy discussion is intended to demonstrate that moving from archaeological data to conclusions, even in the case of a seemingly solid and countable phenomenon like population size, involves a series of assumptions, all of which should continually be reexamined, tested, and where necessary revised. If you, the reader, have an uneasy or skeptical feeling about population estimates after traversing this series of inferential bridges, rest assured that the archaeologist shares your uneasiness. The process of science involves building bridges or even leaping gaps—the important thing is to recognize which bridges are shaky and find ways to make them secure.

To return to the main theme of the chapter, population estimates from Lowland Maya sites (however much you may now distrust them) seem to indicate that more Maya lived in the lowlands than the *milpa* system can support, and that they built considerably larger settlements than are likely with such a system. How can this have been? The answer that will probably seem obvious to most readers—that the Maya used an agricultural system more productive than *milpa*—was not so obvious to archaeologists. The reason lay in an assumption—this time an almost unconscious assumption—that went like this. The *milpa* system is the only farming system used in the Maya lowlands today and is much favored, in fact almost sacred, to farmers. *Therefore* the *milpa* system is the most productive farming system possible and must have been used by the ancient Maya. What no one bothered to ask was whether the *"therefore"* above really follows. What concrete evidence is there that the *milpa* system *is* the most productive system possible? Almost none. In fact, if one asks the question, "How could the Maya have gotten more food from their land than they get from today's *milpa* system?", a whole series of possibilities emerges.

A good point to start in examining more-productive alternatives to the system described above is to question the length of the fallow period, since the very long fallow allowed in the *milpa* system is obviously wasteful of land. What would happen if one attempted to cut this waste by reducing the ratio between farming and fallow? The yields of crops in fields actually under cultivation would almost certainly be less, but enough extra land might be brought under cultivation to result in a net increase in productivity.

The situation might be illustrated by a simple example. Imagine 100 acres of land farmed according to the common modern pattern of 2 years of cropping followed by 6 years of fallow. Of the 100 acres, 12.5 acres would be in first-year *milpa* (freshly cleared after the fallow period), 12.5 acres would be in second-year cropping, and 75 acres would be at various stages of rest. An average yield for first-year *milpa* in the Peten is close to 1500 pounds of corn per acre, while second-year *milpa* should yield about 1000 pounds per acre. Total yield of corn from the 100 acres would be 31,250 pounds. (18,750 from first-year *milpa* and 12,500 from second-year). Assume then that the fallow period is cut from six years to 3 years and that there is a decrease of 20 percent in both first- and second-year yields as a result of the decreased fallow period. With 2 years of cropping and 3 of fallow, the 100 acres would be divided into 20 acres of first-year *milpa* (producing 1200 pounds per acre), 20 acres of second-year *milpa* (producing 800 pounds per acre), and 60 acres under fallow. Total yield from the 100 acres would be 40,000 pounds (24,000 pounds from first-year fields and 16,000 pounds from second-year fields), an increase of 28 percent over the first system. Most of the figures used in these calculations are based on modern production data for *milpa* farming, but one is based on sheer guesswork: the percentage of yield reduction that would result from the reduced amount of fallow. This is, of course, precisely the figure that would determine the viability of the system. If the yield decrease had been 30 percent, rather than the guessed figure of 20 percent, the decreased fallow cycle would have about equaled the original fallow period in yield and would offer no productive advantage.

Another variable in agricultural systems is the amount of labor necessary. Assuming that labor per acre under cultivation does not vary much between 6- and 3-year fallow cycles, the shorter fallow cycle would require 60 percent more labor for the hundred-acre plot than the longer cycle. From the point of view of the individual farmer, the investment of 60 percent more labor to obtain a 28 percent increase in yield would be distinctly uneconomical. But from the standpoint of an overpopulated city-state with a scarcity of land, labor is a cheap commodity, and the shorter fallow cycle would simply mean utilizing people who would otherwise be unemployed and unproductive. The foregoing discussion is intended to demonstrate that we cannot assume that the long fallow cycle used today is necessarily the most productive system in terms of yield per unit of land available. Long-term fallow may instead be only labor efficient, yielding the best return per man hour invested. We need far more experimental studies to provide actual data, but there appears to be a chance that the prehistoric maya might have been able to increase productivity by changing the fallow cycle.

Another means by which the Maya might have been able to achieve higher agricultural productivity per unit of available land is by using crops that give better yields than those used in modern *milpas*. Corn, the present staple, is a marvelous plant—highly productive, nutritious, and almost sacred to the Maya peasant. But there are some plants that will outproduce corn. The yield of root crops such as yams, sweet potatoes, and manioc is extremely high, several times as many pounds per acre as corn. These root crops were known to the Maya and are still grown in small quantities in the Maya area today. Root crops have one disastrous disadvantage, however. They are very low in protein. A survey of the world today suggests that root crops are a successful staple only among people who can add rich sources of animal or fish protein to their diets. Since animal foods are scarce in all parts of the Maya area, root crops could have been used only in areas where fishing or trading for fish was possible.

Work by Dennis Puleston indicates that another candidate as a more productive crop for the Maya is the *ramón* or breadnut tree. The *ramón* tree is native to the rain forest and grows wild over much of the Maya lowlands. Each year during the rainy season the tree produces immense quantities of a sweet and insipid fruit that has little nutritional value. Inside each fruit, however, is a much more promising nut, which can be ground and used in the same manner as ground corn. *Ramón* trees could be easily cultivated and would produce several times as much food per acre as corn. Trees produce for many years, and land planted to *ramón* would never need to be retired for fallow. Finally, the nuts are a good source of vegetable protein and fat, so would make a valuable contribution to the diet. Consequently, if the Maya interspersed *ramón* orchards through their cornfields, or even just had *ramón* groves around their houses, the addition to food supplies would have been substantial. There is at least a hint that the prehistoric Maya cultivated *ramón* in the fact that the concentration of the trees is suspiciously high in the modern vegetation around archaeological sites.

Another route by which the ancient Maya could have significantly raised food production would have been by farming the low-lying seasonal swamps or *bajos* that dot the landscape of the Peten. *Bajo* lands make up about 50 percent of the total area of the Maya Classic heartlands, and all calculations of the number of people the area could feed are based upon the assumption that *bajos* made no contribution to food production. Modern farmers studiously avoid *bajos* (it is difficult and decidedly unproductive to grow corn in six inches of water) but any system that would make them usable would tap a large reservoir of unused land.

Archaeologists have recently discovered indications of a technique used by prehistoric peoples to make swamplands available for farming. This consists of building ridged-field systems in which dirt is piled up to make ridges that are high enough to avoid destructive amounts of moisture. Although remains of ridged-field systems are mostly located in South America, some have been discovered along the Rio Candelaria at the western edge of the Maya lowlands. There is still no evidence that would indicate whether the system was ever used extensively in the Peten swamplands, but investigation of the problem is certainly called for.

Using the possibilities just discussed, it would be easy to construct on paper an agricultural system that would be considerably more productive per available acre than the *milpa* system. The difficulty now lies in finding a way to test archaeologically whether such a system was used. The problems of testing are very severe. Food materials are never preserved in the steamy climate of the rain forest. Chemical changes in the soil that might be induced by different farming techniques would long since have been erased by natural process. Analysis of ancient pollen will not help detect root crops, which leave no pollen, or *ramón* trees, whose pollen is abundant as part of the natural vegetation whether they were used or not. The means to test the prehistoric subsistence system, if they are ever discovered, will probably come from the ever-increasing sophistication of chemists and physicists, whose techniques have already made so many unexpected contributions to archaeology. In the meantime, we must remain in the uncomfortable Alice-in-Wonderland world where ideas can be endlessly debated but never resolved, because there is no way to find out which side is right.

Now that Maya alternatives to the *milpa* system have been outlined, we must look more closely at the concept of productivity. The emphasis has been upon finding an agricultural system that would be more productive than *milpa*. But "productive" is a relative term and has no meaning unless the kind of productivity is specified. At least three different measures of productivity are applicable to the present case: productivity per unit of *available land*, productivity per unit of *land under cultivation*, and productivity per unit *of labor*. These three measures need not operate in the same fashion; all may go up or down together, or they may go in different directions. In the example of changing the fallow cycle presented earlier, a shortened fallow cycle would increase productivity for the total acreage available, but would decrease yield per acre under cultivation and sharply reduce yield per man-hour. On the other hand, the substitution of *ramón* trees for corn would probably increase all three kinds of productivity.

Our concern so far has been with productivity per unit of

land available, or its converse, total food obtainable given a fixed amount of land. This measure is the one that a political system must maximize if it is to prosper. Imagine a hypothetical Maya city-state of the Classic period with control of a territory of 100 square kilometers. The territory would be carefully delimited and surrounded by land owned by neighboring communities; expansion would be impossible without a major commitment to warfare and conquest. To achieve prosperity in foodstuffs or to feed an increasing population, the task of the rulers would be to get as many pounds of food as possible from these 100 square kilometers. Crops and techniques, the amount of land under cultivation, and the amount of labor invested are variables— items that can be changed to obtain more total food.

During the Classic period, Maya political units must have had fixed territories and high populations. There were probably worsening problems in finding land that could be farmed by a growing populace. In such situations, labor is cheap and there is an incentive to invest it lavishly on projects of low productive return.

But what of the poor peasant? We have been looking at productivity through the eyes of the leaders whose interest is in total production rather than in the rewards to the laborer for his work, and what is good for the state need not necessarily coincide with what the low-class worker considers to be to his advantage. The laborer obviously would like enough to eat and, in addition, would like a surplus to trade for things that he finds desirable. Beyond a certain point, however, the investment of more labor for extra surplus is no longer worth the effort. The peasant, when the work load gets too heavy, can forego luxuries —the fancy wedding for his daughter, an extra curing ceremony, the fiesta offering to the gods—whether or not this forbearance is in the best interests of the state. The problem of state leaders is to make sure that this point of relaxation of effort does not come too soon and result in the irreparable loss of surpluses needed for state purposes.

The potential lack of correspondence between the wishes of the peasant and the needs of the total system leads to questioning another old assumption about prehistoric Maya farming— the assumption that the Maya agricultural system needed little management from the leaders of the society. Maya agriculture was usually contrasted with systems that constructed large irrigation works and neeeded to organize, control, and direct immense labor crews to build and maintain dikes and canals. By comparison, the Maya peasant, merely engaged in slashing and burning his *milpa,* was like a self-winding watch. He knew the techniques, needed no more labor help than could be provided by his family, and without any directions produced the highest yield the land was capable of producing.

I hope that this picture already sounds suspiciously at variance with the view of Maya agriculture I have been trying to develop. I *do believe* that the peasant, if left to his own devices, would have engaged in an agriculture not unlike the modern *milpa* system. After all, this probably provides the highest yield per man hour of labor—a point that is a matter of no small concern to the man who has to do the work. I *do not believe*, however, that this was the best the land could produce nor that this system was in the best interests of the Maya political unit and its leaders. To maximize production of the overall unit did require management—careful planning and balancing of crops sown and the length of fallow cycles, as well as distribution plans to get the right foodstuffs to the right people. The peasant had to be induced to cooperate—to invest increased labor to reach the level of production the state needed. What the inducements were will become evident when we turn to discussions of trade and social organization.

5. The Economic System

Some theorists, who see economics as the sole driving force of society, seem to picture man as a combination computer and robot, turning automatically toward any source that promises economic gain and away from all else. I would be unhappy to go to this extreme and to imagine that the whole of Maya culture, complete with priests and temples and astronomical calculations, could be completely understood by an analysis of the mechanisms of production and consumption. Yet I do believe that the economic structure was more of a mainspring in Maya society than has usually been claimed, and consider economics to be worth discussing as one of the first topics in this book.

As was true for subsistence, the Maya economic system has traditionally been viewed as uncomplicated. The peasants were a happy, carefree lot with few and simple wants, while the elite were satisfied with some peasant labor and a few imported trinkets. One could almost imagine the Maya—had the opportunity arisen—selling a ceremonial center for a box of imported beads and a few blankets. The reason for this simplistic view again lay in assumptions about the rain forest environment. The rain forest was homogeneous—so the argument went—and its resources were free for the taking. Each family could fulfill its own needs, so there were few products to trade and little use for markets or means to distribute goods. Long-distance trade involved only luxury items for the elite, items of high value and small bulk that could be imported with minimal transportation facilities.

Again the story—theoretically pleasing though it may be—does not stand up well in the light of archaeological fact. We know that pottery during the Classic period was produced in specialized manufacturing centers and was not something each housewife put together during the off-hours in her household routine (Figure 14). By Late Classic times, about one-third of the pottery used in the average household at Tikal was of richly painted polychrome types, the product of lavish expenditure of skilled labor. Other crafts were probably the results of similar centralized production. Evidence from Maya paintings and sculpture and the rare chance find of an occasional perishable artifact that has endured the ravages of the tropical climate show a rich variety of carved and painted wooden objects, while Maya art portrays a gaudy display of clothing in myriad colors and designs. Without quantities of the objects themselves for study, we can never be sure that these things may not all have been homemade, but the variety and good workmanship that is evi-

Figure 14

Maya Potter. *Among the Maya Indians of today, pottery is still manufactured by the same methods used in the Classic period. It is also still a specialized craft, for particular villages are pottery-making centers that supply large areas with their products. (Arizona State Museum, University of Arizona, William Holland Collection.)*

dent even in painted representations of them does not suggest an every-man-for-himself system of production.

In picturing the Maya economic system, I am more comfortable imagining parallels to our own society, in which even poor families depend on manufacturers and distributors to supply items for their household use, than I am in envisioning similarities between the Maya and those simple cultures in which all products are gathered, hunted, or grown and then ground, gouged, spun, or sewn by each family in a veritable orgy of self-sufficiency.

In other words, I think the Maya had a complex economic system involving extensive interdependence among people with different occupations. Parallels to our own economic system certainly did not extend, however, to the point of an industrial, mass-production economy. Although the Maya had sacrificed economic self-sufficiency, the system of specialization they employed probably operated on a small scale and along with continued involvement of many people in agricultural pursuits. The prehistoric system may have been similar to the sort of specialization that still exists in Maya villages in highland Guatemala. There each village turns out a particular kind of product —one will make pottery; another, hats; a third, shoes; and so on. At the same time, most people continue to be *milpa* farmers and practice their specialties during lax moments of the agricultural cycle. Thus, as far as the total economic situation goes, there is quite an intricate pattern of specialization but one that includes few people who devote full time to their specialty.

And what of the economics of food supplies? Most of the Maya people probably did at least some farming. Should we interpret this to mean that almost everyone grew his own food and there was little need for the economy to deal in foodstuffs? This is what has usually been assumed, but, as should already be obvious, I have little intention of letting old assumptions go unchallenged. Again, there is room for doubt. Everyone, of course, will readily agree that there was at least a small group of upper-class rulers and specialists who got their food from public support rather than by their own production. (Who could imagine, for instance, the high priest of Tikal Temple I picking worms off his own corn plants?) But this elite corps need not have been large—a few hundred, perhaps, at most ceremonial centers and a few thousand at the largest sites—and could have been easily supported if each farmer was producing a small surplus.

But the problem would take on quite different aspects if larger numbers of specialists had to be supported. It would then become a balance-of-payments problem for the very large sites that were scattered at intervals throughout the lowlands. Were these largest of Maya centers still self-sufficient units in food production, or had they, at least by the end of Classic times, reached the point at which a regular deficit in food production forced them to import supplies from more-productive (or less-populated) regions? The question is a fundamental one, since a state budget with a planned deficit in local food production opens new and self-stimulating economic vistas. The heavily populated centers where such budgets would have occurred were areas where land shortages and low crop yields per man-hour of labor would have made it very difficult to increase food production. At the same time, these centers would have enjoyed a heavy concentration of specialists and managerial talent and a large labor pool, all of which were resources that could have been used to advantage in emphasizing manufacturing and craft production instead of agriculture. For the worker, craft production is usually more profitable than farming, particularly when the agricultural system is becoming more labor consuming. The history of urban development in this century is ample demonstration of the attractions that city work opportunities have for a rural population.

For the government, diverting labor from agricultural pursuits into channels of specialized production can prove a very profitable enterprise as long as markets for the products can be uncovered and distribution systems to get products to the markets are created. But the government that chooses this course is also choosing increased vulnerability. It must rely on outsiders—on potentially undependable alliances and extended supply routes—for its ultimate necessity, food for its specialists and citizens. If some Maya centers were shifting to more specialized economies and counting on imported food, the traditional picture of Maya trade and economic interaction would be drastically altered. Rather than a low-volume flow of trade in luxury items for elite use, the trade would have involved large quantities of foodstuffs and the products exchanged for them. The proposed heavy trade in foodstuffs within the lowlands would have added to the substantial import trade in salt, obsidian, and volcanic stone discussed earlier. To move such vast quantities of bulk goods would have demanded a quite different system from that needed for procurement of the low-volume, elite-only goods previously considered to constitute the majority of long-distance commerce. We must now think of vast forces of sweating porters moving tons of material along jungle trails. Inherent in the system was the need to marshal large quantities of manpower, to organize procurement and distribution schedules, and to make the appropriate political and economic arrangements to secure goods and arrange for passage through a maze of political boundaries. Among the Maya elite class there must have been skillful and hardworking experts— prehistoric Rothschilds and Rockefellers—and their staffs, who wheeled and dealed in major commodities markets. This is a far cry from the picture of a nonfunctional elite class idly engaged in making astronomical calculations and conducting occasional ceremonies for the edification of the peasants.

Whether or not markets played an important role in the Classic Maya economy is another important question. We know that in highland Mexico there was a wonderful market at the Aztec capital of Tenochtitlan when the Spanish arrived. The Conquistador Bernal Díaz described it at length and marveled at the variety of goods and the thorough organization, complete with tax collectors and judges to arbitrate disputes. But sources that describe the Maya of the Conquest period are strangely silent about markets; certainly nothing approaching the grandeur of the Tenochtitlan market could have been viewed by the Spaniards in Yucatan (Figure 15).

It is possible that the Maya of both Conquest and Classic times distributed products through some means other than market exchange. Peoples in many parts of the world used, or still use, what are called *redistributive systems*, in which goods are collected by a central authority (a chief or government, depending on cultural level) and then parceled out again to those who need them. Such systems provide tight control of the population, since everyone depends on the state to provide items he needs. They also have the advantage of splashy and very obvious chances to demonstrate to people how nice it is to have a government. Redistributive systems result in very high tax rates and usually involve state control of the people who make specialty items. To decide what sort of economy the Classic Maya had—markets, redistribution, or some mixture—is an extremely important issue but one that will not be easy to resolve. The solution will demand deciding what differences in the archaeological record would result from the possible alternatives and then doing research to seek out the crucial facts.

The message in all the foregoing considerations is that the Classic Maya had the complex kind of economic system we expect of a civilized society. Specialization, long-distance trade, concentration of capital in the hands of the elite class, and rewards for the lower classes in the form of tangible benefits rather than spiritual blessings created an integrated system the parts of which worked according to solid economic principles. The old model of the Maya as an economic anomaly with few understandable ties between upper and lower classes need no longer be a source of archaeological vexation.

Figure 15

Maya Indian Market. *Markets are an age-old institution among the Maya Indians of highland regions, like the Indians in Chiapas, Mexico. Whether or not markets were well developed among the Classic Maya of the lowlands, however, is still an unresolved question. (Arizona State Museum, University of Arizona, William Holland Collection.)*

6. Social and Political Organization

That cultures are systems is a basic premise of this book. Societies could not survive and thrive if they were random collections of individuals, each pursuing his own ends oblivious to everyone else. Complex societies characteristically consist of people who differ from each other in occupation, in amount of possessions, and in degree of power and authority. But the operation, and even the existence, of the overall society depends on mutual aid and cooperation between people in diverse social roles. Furthermore, since altruism is not a reliable characteristic of personal interaction, the cooperation and mutual aid must be built into the very fabric of social institutions so that roles leave litlle chance that the system will fail through adverse individual decisions.

This is perhaps an overcomplicated way of saying that cultures depend on regularities in the ways that people behave toward each other. Even in living societies where behavior can be observed in all its bewildering variety, the anthropologists' job of constructing rules and reasons for human interaction is staggering. For extinct cultures from which only imperishable objects remain, the difficulties are immeasurably greater. Yet just as I have tried to reconstruct the operation of the Maya economic system, I must also try to resurrect models of long-vanished social and political institutions.

The kinds of information available for the archaeologist to use in the Herculean labor of reconstructing ancient social systems include such things as the form and location of structures, the nature of tool assemblages, and the offerings that accompany burials. Since the Maya had a well-developed representational art, they have left the welcome addition of paintings and carvings in which they portrayed themselves and their activities. Finally, the Maya were a literate people, and their still mostly undeciphered inscriptions give fascinating hints of historical individuals and their activities.

A good place to start the consideration of Maya social organization is with the units that are suggested by the arrangement of structures within the ruins. In order to say something about the smallest units of social organization, it is necessary to turn to the evidence provided by the mapping and excavation of the small platforms upon which the Maya built their houses. Everywhere in the Maya lowlands where house platforms have been investigated, the platforms occur in small clusters of three to six structures placed around the edges of open plazas. This pattern strongly suggests that the basic social unit of the Maya was the extended family, composed of an older couple and their children, both married and unmarried. The extended family is the standard unit among modern Maya, and the housing compounds of such families almost exactly duplicate the layout of the prehistoric house groups. Archaeologically, one of the platforms in a group is frequently somewhat larger or more elegant than the others. These larger platforms were probably the residences of family heads, who today still tend to be patriarchal in their dealings with junior members of the family. Excavation often shows that some of the houses in a compound were added at a later date than the initial structures, as would be the case if children married and started their own households within the family compound. Although there is no concrete evidence that the residents of prehistoric housemound clusters actually *were* members of extended families, the analogy with the modern situation is so striking that there is little reason to doubt the conclusion.

The household groups themselves are clustered into larger units that form hamlets or small villages in rural areas or what look like neighborhoods in large sites. These next largest aggregates (termed "zones" by William Bullard) would have housed a hundred to a few hundred people. A community or neighborhood of this size needs services and administration, and almost always a small ceremonial precinct is found within a zone, as are small masonry structures of palace type that probably were used by local elite. Exactly what kind of social group resided in these zones is less certain than for housemound clusters. Many anthropologists feel that each zone housed a large kinship group such as a clan, so that all of the inhabitants of the zone would have considered themselves related and would have functioned as a unit because of kinship ties and obligations. I have serious doubts about this interpretation and would prefer to imagine zones in which the ties were primarily territorial and administrative without much dependence on kinship organization above the level of extended families. Whatever may be the case, no archaeological evidence gathered so far permits testing hypotheses about the organizational principles of zones.

Although zones must have offered some community services to residents, even zones located in rural areas can hardly have been independent of, or complete without, larger centers. Maya society was far too complex for peasants not to feel the need for the manufactured goods and social opportunities offered by the semiurban ceremonial centers. Looked at from the other side, the larger communities could not have survived without the labor and food production of the lower classes, so they would hardly have tolerated independence of peasant communities. Within the confines of the major centers, it is easy to imagine zone neighborhoods as the counterparts of modern political wards or religious parishes. Villages in the hinterlands may have been the homes of minor local nobles (undoubtedly subservient to the leaders of the center) or may have been the direct creation of the larger centers, established to aid contact with and exploitation of the farming population. None of the zone-size centers have hieroglyphic inscriptions, suggesting both that their elite were not important enough to rate commemoration and that they could not afford the highly specialized skills of the stone-carver and scribe.

The next larger unit, the major ceremonial center (Figure 16), is the key to understanding the upper levels of Maya society. Major centers occur 10 to 20 miles apart throughout the lowlands. They invariably include central areas with the architectural masterpieces that typify Maya culture. In such sites there are carved hieroglyphic inscriptions, and each site had its own emblem glyph. Major sites also had ball courts where the Maya played a ceremonial game that involved hitting a large rubber ball without using either hands or feet. We can picture major centers as hubs of economic networks and centers for the rural hamlets and villages in the surrounding countryside. Specialized services, manufacturing, and ceremonies of great pomp in the centers drew crowds of visitors from surrounding areas and consumed vast quantities of energy and goods in the service of the gods and the upper classes.

A question that has been debated with the production of considerable heat and not much light is whether or not Maya ceremonial centers should be classified as cities. The city is a characteristic form that occurs only in civilized societies. Two features that define cities are size and population density. Populations must number in the thousands (a minimum of 10,000 people is a frequently mentioned figure), and the inhabitants must be so tightly clustered that densities per square mile number in excess of 1000 people. Most Maya centers fail to meet these criteria, for their population densities usually fall

Figure 16

The Ceremonial Center at Copan. *This reconstruction of the central part of Copan, Honduras, by Tatiana Proskouriakoff shows how a major ceremonial center might have appeared during its heyday. Dominated by massive temple-pyramids, the center also contains structures for administration and elite residence, as well as vast plazas in which the populace must have gathered on days of feasts and ceremonies. (The Peabody Museum, Harvard University.)*

well below 1000 per square mile. Consequently, Maya culture is not infrequently cited as a "civilization without cities." Although some Mayanists feel incensed that the urbane Maya should be nonurban, I am happy to agree with the prevailing opinion that the Maya were not cityfolk.

The justice of this judgment becomes evident when Tikal is compared with Teotihuacan, which in the first centuries of the Christian era was one of the world's greatest cities (see Figures 17 and 18). Teotihuacan had 100,000 inhabitants packed one upon another, as in the densest of modern cities. More than seven square miles at the center of Teotihuacan were filled with continuous construction, the wall of one structure abutting the wall of the structure next door. The only open spaces were streets and narrow alleys. One could probably have walked for hours on end through Teotihuacan without ever setting foot off a paved surface or even seeing a tree or plant except for those

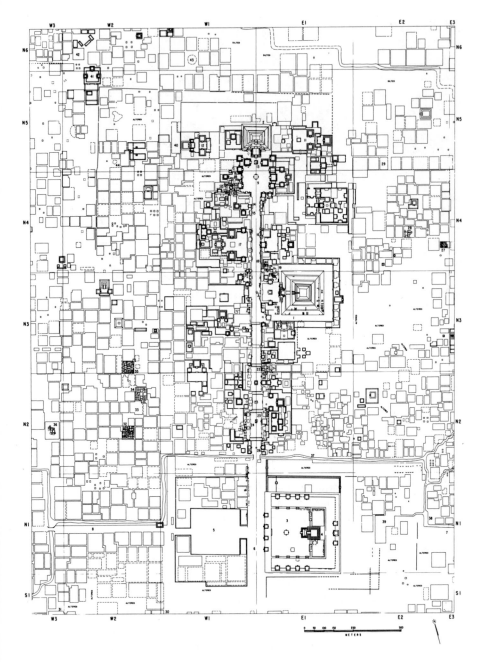

Figure 17

Map of Teotihuacan. *Note the careful rectangular planning and the continuous construction that leaves almost no open space in this central Mexican city. (Courtesy of René Millon. All rights reserved.)*

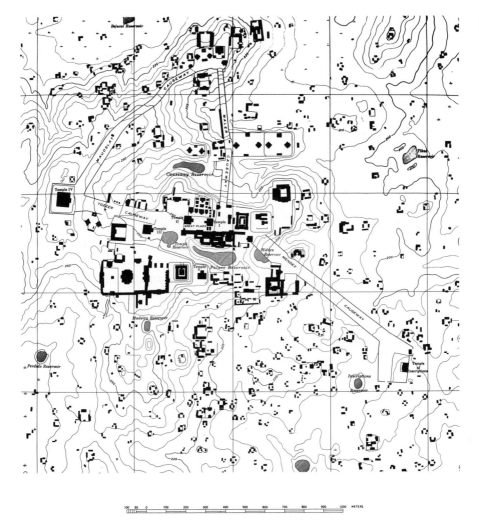

Figure 18

Map of Tikal. *The settlement pattern of Tikal contrasts strikingly with that of Teotihuacan. Like most Maya sites, Tikal shows relatively scattered settlement and lacks the strict block patterning that characterizes Teotihuacan. (The University Museum, University of Pennsylvania.)*

kept in pots like the sadly hopeful window-box gardens of twentieth-century apartment dwellers. Comparing this with Tikal, sprinkled with garden patches and groves of *ramón* trees, is convincing evidence of fundamental differences between the two sites. But one must remember that Tikal in Late Classic times was by no means a "vacant town," in spite of its scattered settlement pattern. At least 10,000 people lived within a half hour's walk of the "downtown" area (certainly no farther in terms of time than most Americans are from their own centers). Father away, but still within the political and economic sphere of Tikal, lived another 15,000 to 30,000 people, all of whom must have been frequent visitors to the central area. Teotihuacan and Tikal were both centers for large numbers of people, but they were centers with very different configurations and must accordingly have faced different problems. Crowding, sanitation, and the price of housing must have plagued inhabitants of Teotihuacan. While the more scattered settlement of Tikal residents would have avoided these problems, it must have done so at the expense of communication, ease of access to central services, and efficiency in policing the population.

The foregoing outline of Maya communities leaves many questions unanswered. What social roles were present in Maya society? How were wealth and prestige distributed? Was social mobility possible, or was a Maya doomed to spend his life in the social class in which he was born? Questions like these are difficult to answer because archaeology produces little evidence that can be directly converted to answers about social position. It is possible to make inferences from data now available, but the difficult process of checking these inferences against further data remains to be undertaken.

Any society rests upon the hands and energy of a laboring class. Among the Maya, as in most early civilizations, the bulk of the laborers were involved in food production. Certainly the majority of the small unembellished house platforms, particularly those in rural areas, must have belonged to peasant farmers. A not uncommon popular view of social divisions in early civilization (to be seen in glowing color in many Hollywood epics) is that peasants were downtrodden masses, giving their all in goods and labor to support cruel and haughty leaders and gaining little but punishments and imprecations in return. But archaeological evidence will not support such a view of Maya class interactions. Maya house platforms were neat and well constructed, and plazas were carefully paved. Even lower-class residential areas must have presented a pleasant, semirural appearance. House clusters were far enough apart to leave room between for gardens or groves of useful trees. Even though the virgin forest may have been largely cut over, the leafy green shade of tropical vegetation was probably preserved as shelter from the sun. Objects procured from specialized centers of manufacture abounded in peasant households. By Late Classic times even the most remote households regularly used hand-painted polychrome pottery for serving food, and the vessels used for domestic routines like food storage and carrying water were the products of specialized manufacturers. Every peasant housewife ground corn with implements of hard stone imported for her from sources many days distant. This evidence certainly points to an economy of abundance for the working classes rather than the dismal, poverty-stricken fate so often assigned them in fiction.

The concept of a relatively prosperous peasantry makes it easier to envision why Maya society held together. Many demands were made on the lower classes by an elite that was expanding in size and becoming more ambitious in the projects that they undertook. In the traditional view of Maya society, the elite have been pictured as rather ineffective intellectuals who devoted most of their time to esoteric considerations of gods and calendars. Yet it is not very clear why, in such a situation, the uneducated masses should have bothered to respond to incessant calls for more goods and more labor. General prosperity—and moreover a prosperity in which the elite directed trade and specialized manufacture—is a believable motivation. It would now seem that the peasant, too, had a stake in the system. The supply of things that he used and needed depended on the state of the national economy, and, as any present day politician can testify, a system that returns a satisfyingly high level of tangible rewards is greeted with general enthusiasm. Nevertheless, religious sentiments, although admittedly overemphasized in some past attempts to explain the operation of Maya culture, should not be overlooked. All indications are that the Maya were a deeply religious people, extremely interested in the supernatural and convinced that gods and stars and planets brought good or ill fortune into their lives. A firm belief that placating supernatural powers can bring rewards reinforces further efforts—the gods can be an investment, particularly when they are inextricably interwoven with the powers that also control the economy.

Gain of status and prestige can also be a reward for which men will expend incredible energy. Evon Z. Vogt, a cultural anthropologist who has worked with Maya Indians in Chiapas, Mexico, has suggested a scheme that would provide both a reason—gain of prestige—and a mechanism—a system of rotating offices like the modern *cargo* system—for social integration among the prehistoric Maya. As it operates today, the *cargo* system consists of a series of political and religious offices (cargos) that are filled by volunteers who serve one-year terms. The offices are ranked, and an individual must begin by serving in a low-level position before he is eligible to move to more important posts. Office holding is an expensive business; the incumbent must finance ceremonies and fiestas associated with his office at a cost that may run to several times annual income for the higher-level positions. The only reward for participation is prestige and community status, but this by itself is enough that some villages have long waiting lists of people who have volunteered years in advance for the most important cargos.

I find no difficulty in accepting the possibility of a Classic-period cargo system. It would not have replaced the aristocracy nor applied to positions demanding great skill or long training —one can hardly imagine a country bumpkin coming to the center for a year to calculate astronomical cycles or carve glyphs. But one can easily envision ceremonials with hundreds of simple tasks, such as carrying sacred images in a procession or holding an offering, each of which might have conferred a touch of greatness and prestige. If each job holder was expected to make a "contribution" to the expense of the festivities, a sort of voluntary and painless tax on ceremonies, income for the directors would be large. And, of course, everyone who participated and gained status thereby would be inevitably drawn to praise the importance and merits of the system. One can picture all of the members of a satellite community working madly to finance their local leader for a term in the nearby major center and then basking for years in the reflected glory. Probably everyone has witnessed enough send-our-band-to-the-state-championships campaigns so that the system will not seem too remote. There is no reason why economic rewards could not also be built in as reinforcing mechanisms. The distribution to cargo holders of long-range trade items gathered by the central authorities would serve both to solve problems of allocation and to contribute to the strength of the entire system. A cargo system then, could have been a useful part of social integration in the Classic period, and the present system may, indeed, be a survival from far earlier times.

The foregoing paragraphs attempt to delineate reasons why lower-class Maya would willingly have participated in the socioeconomic system that supported the upper classes. Inequalities and class struggles are important topics, but they are social pathologies; knowledge of them does not contribute to understanding how societies succeed. The Maya were a successful society for many centuries, so we must seek to understand the mechanisms that smoothed the rough edges of social inter-

action and bound people of different kinds together in working
for mutually satisfactory goals.

But Maya Classic society consisted of far more than humble
peasants and mighty lords; there is ample evidence to suggest
a complex social pyramid above the level of lower-class workers.
The zone centers described in previous pages are indicative of
what seems to be a middle-class population. Examples of these
centers have been carefully investigated at Tikal by Marshall
Becker. They prove to be, in many respects, miniature versions
of the great structural groupings at the site center. The heart
of a neighborhood cluster is a formal plaza surrounded by
structures. On the east edge of the plaza there is invariably a
ceremonial pyramid that is a direct, but much smaller, copy of
the giant temple pyramids described earlier. A few pyramids in
the wealthier neighborhoods are topped by tiny stone temples
that are, like the substructures, miniature copies of those in the
center. Most neighborhood pyramids, however, lack surmounting masonry structures and were probably crowned by temples
of perishable materials. Pyramids that have been excavated
prove to have been frequently rebuilt, refinished, and enlarged.
Associated with each rebuilding was a burial, usually placed in a
pit or small chamber beneath the central stairway. This pattern,
which is mirrored on a much more grandiose scale in temple
tomb burials, probably marks the ceremonies associated with
the death of one local leader and accession of a successor. The
new person in charge evidently oversaw the interment of his
predecessor with appropriate pomp and circumstance and then
repaired the damage caused by opening a burial shaft and established his claim to public works by building a new structure.

A second fundamental feature of neighborhood centers is
one or more palace-type structures ranged around the local
plaza. There is variation in the number, size, and elegance of
these structures, apparently in relation to the importance and
wealth of the neighborhood. Some of the smaller centers seemingly could not afford full masonry palaces but made do with
stone walls about half room height, which were presumably
topped by upper walls and roofs of perishable materials. Other
groups have several structures of carefully finished masonry.
Local leaders probably used these structures in their functions
as part of the administrative and bureaucratic organizations
that governed the site.

The neighborhood units must have been an integral part of
organizational structure. The leaders of the units probably
had responsibility for unenviable jobs like gathering taxes, supplies, and labor forces for the upper classes. Local centers

may have supplied some services, such as small-scale religious ceremonies, and might also have been the final distribution point for trade goods and manufactured items controlled by the elite. It is impossible to determine whether each neighborhood group possessed areas of farming land, but there are archaeological hints that some groups had craft specialties. Debris from one such center at Tikal contained an unusual concentration of ceramic specialty items (*incensarios* and curtain holders were particularly abundant) indicating that the center was probably a pottery-making unit. Other units that yielded immense concentrations of figurines may have been involved in figurine manufacture or use.

Atop the Maya social pyramid were a series of great lords, about whom there is more information than about any other social class. These are the individuals whose portraits were carved on stone or painted in multicolored murals and whose great deeds are proclaimed in the hieroglyphic inscriptions we are only beginning to understand. The meanings of enough glyphs have now been determined so that it is possible to interpret some of the historical information recorded in stone carvings. The names of individuals occur as long strings of glyphs, which must include both personal names and the honorable titles that royalty of all nations tend to accumulate. Other glyphs refer to events. There is, for instance, a glyph that is always associated with the earliest date given for a ruler and must refer to his birth or to some ceremony shortly thereafter. Another, known as an ascension glyph, seems to indicate the date at which a ruler took office, since it usually occurs on stelae showing a king seated on a throne to which a stairway or ladder traversed by a set of footprints lead. There are also glyphs that represent "capture" or "captor of" and "death of." The inscriptions indicate that each major Maya site had a single ruler, who ruled for life and was succeeded by a son or other close relative. Although the rulers were almost invariably men, women are often portrayed in the carvings and seem to have exercised considerable influence in the affairs of state. Rulers are pictured involved in military, religious, and diplomatic activities in which, not surprisingly, they are always successful and from which they emerge covered with still greater glory.

An example of the career of a particular ruler will help to illustrate the multifarious activities to which the mighty among the Maya dedicated themselves. Miss Tatiana Proskouriakoff, who more than anyone else is responsible for the breakthrough in historic interpretation of Maya texts, has documented a particularly complete and interesting record for a man we know as Bird Jaguar, who ruled at the site of Yaxchilan in the eighth century of our era. Bird Jaguar was born in A.D. 709 and was related to a man known as Shield Jaguar, who was then ruler of Yaxchilan. His relationship to Shield Jaguar was a matter either of pride or of concern to Bird Jaguar, since he emphasizes it repeatedly in his inscriptions and also seems to claim descent from several earlier Jaguar rulers. Bird Jaguar gives the impression of protesting too much about the glories of his ancestry, which, coupled with a suspicious gap between Shield Jaguar's death and Bird Jaguar's accession to power, suggests that Bird Jaguar's path to the throne may have been far from uncomplicated. Power struggles within the inner circles of palaces are commonplace in societies where rule is confined to a tiny hereditary group, and there are hints that such a power struggle may have occurred after the death of Shield Jaguar. A period of ten years passed during which no inscriptions clearly name a ruler of Yaxchilan, although a woman who had probably been a consort of Shield Jaguar and one or two dubiously identified males seem to have been involved in the political picture. Then in A.D. 752 Bird Jaguar took office—an event many times celebrated in later inscriptions.

Early achievements of Bird Jaguar had a distinctly military tone. Yaxchilan Stela 11 depicts him (a year before his accession) accepting homage from three kneeling prisoners (see Figure 19). Three years after taking the throne, Bird Jaguar achieved a triumph that was to be remembered throughout his career. Yaxchilan Lintel 8 (Figure 20) portrays the victory and tells of it in an inscribed text. The lintel shows Bird Jaguar and a companion in the act of subjugating two other Maya lords. Bird Jaguar's victim has a name glyph consisting of a skull outlined by dots, which gives rise to our designation of him as Jeweled Skull. The event was of such importance that it became incorporated as part of Bird Jaguar's title, for he is frequently referred to in later inscriptions as Captor of Jeweled Skull.

These scenes and inscriptions demonstrate several features important to an understanding of Maya politics. Leadership at arms was clearly an important duty of rulers. That people were captured or surrendered in military engagements is evident. We are uncertain, however, who the captives were, although some of them were obviously men of rank. Both their names and their faces proclaim them as Maya, but whether capitulation signifies the defeat of other major centers or simply minor consolidation within a local area is uncertain. It does not seem likely, though, that rulers would so proudly proclaim victory in local skirmishes —a mighty king does not boast of enemies in his own backyard.

Figure 19

Bird Jaguar on Stela 11, Yaxchilan. *This scene,
which took place in* A.D. *751, shows Bird
Jaguar receiving submission from three lords
who kneel before him. Since the date of this
event was a year before Bird Jaguar succeeded
to the throne of Yaxchilan, it may commemorate a struggle or ceremony related to his rise
to power. (From* The Rise and Fall of Maya
Civilization, *by J. Eric S. Thompson. Copyright 1954, 1966 by the University of Oklahoma Press.)*

Figure 20

Bird Jaguar on Lintel 8, Yaxchilan. *Here, the Maya have commemo-
rated a conquest in which Bird Jaguar subdues a lord called Jeweled
Skull, from the name glyph on his thigh. An unnamed companion of
Bird Jaguar, to his left, captures a second prisoner. (Courtesy Tatiana
Proskouriakoff.)*

Even if we conclude that other major centers were defeated,
we still do not know whether this led to occupation and govern-
ing of one center by another or whether peace was reestablished
by a payoff of goods or territory without interference in the
autonomy of the vanquished center.

To return to the career of Bird Jaguar, his reign seems to
have become peaceful after the martial outbursts near the time
of his inauguration. A series of carvings and inscriptions from
later in his career record important sacred rites. Ceremonies
involving snakes occur (snake handling is frequently depicted
among the Maya) and scenes showing self-sacrificial bloodletting. Bird Jaguar is only once pictured as personally involved
in the ceremonies, but several women associated with his rule

appear as celebrants. These scenes indicate the importance of ceremonials in the life of the ancient Maya and the high status of women in sacred matters.

Another series of carvings shows Bird Jaguar interacting with other important individuals. In a theme that occurs on several monuments, Bird Jaguar faces a woman who bears an enigmatic bundle. Several interpretations of this scene are possible, but Miss Proskouriakoff believes that it represents the arrangement of a marriage contract and that the bundle symbolizes the bride's dowry. On one lintel, Bird Jaguar is shown exchanging staffs with a young man, while other carvings show less well-defined interactions with other men. The substance of these carvings suggests that Bird Jaguar was hard at work cementing alliances with important groups from other sites. Several of the individuals with whom Bird Jaguar deals have a moon glyph as part of their names, and Miss Proskouriakoff believes that this Moon-sign Family was the ruling lineage in some area important to Yaxchilan. In the long run, the arrangements with the Moon-sign Family seem not to have worked well for Yaxchilan (or perhaps worked too well for the Moon-sign people), for a generation after Bird Jaguar's death, a Moon-sign man seems to have become ruler of Yaxchilan.

A superb painted vase from the site of Altar de Sacrificios (Figure 21) supplies another exciting example of interaction among the Maya elite. Richard E. W. Adams, who analyzed the pottery from Altar de Sacrificios, believes that the Altar Vase depicts funeral rites of a middle-aged woman buried in an important tomb in Altar Structure A-III. Six figures appear in the scene, two of them dancing and the rest engaged in what seem to be other kinds of ceremonial activities. Each figure is accompanied by an identifying panel of hieroglyphs, and the accuracy in representation of the drawings leaves little doubt that specific individuals are portrayed. The dancer dressed in jaguar-skin tights has a glyph panel that includes the emblem glyph of Yaxchilan and another glyph that suggests that he is either the ruler Bird Jaguar or his representative. The chubby, seated gentleman holding a jar is identified by his glyphs as being from Tikal, from which he presumably brings offerings. Neither name nor place glyphs of any of the other figures can be identified, but the burial offerings give reason to suspect that an emissary from the Guatemalan highlands was present at the funeral. Since Altar de Sacrificios is not a very imposing site, it is interesting that death rites for a member of its nobility were attended by representatives from two of the most important centers in the Late Classic lowlands. Although nothing so wonderfully explicit as the Altar Vase has been recovered elsewhere, the offerings from major tombs at Tikal hint that visitors from all over Mesoamerica may have attended, or at least have sent offerings to ceremonies conducted for the rulers of really important centers.

These data provide a glimpse of the intensity and complexity of interactions between major political powers in the Maya lowlands. Sometimes at war with each other, at other times bound by fragile pacts of mutual friendship and cooperation, the centers remained forever in competition for power and resources. Hot and cold wars, brinkmanship, and detente, it seems, are not really inventions of twentieth-century politicians. Among the Maya, international bargaining was further complicated by the existence of complex marital networks that must have woven royal families together in a tangled web like the one familiar to anyone who has studied the history of European royalty.

We come now to the question of the ultimate size of Maya political units. There is no problem in identifying major cere-monial centers as units—the buildings in a center are contiguous to each other and separated from those of other centers, and we can read the name glyphs of the sites in inscriptions. It has frequently been suggested that each Maya ceremonial center was an independent city-state, so that the Maya lowlands

Figure 21

Altar Vase. *This painted vase, from a burial at the site of Altar de Sacrificios, is thought to depict actual funeral ceremonies of the eighth century. (The Peabody Museum, Harvard University.)*

would have been like the Greece of Homeric days, divided into
small kingdoms, each centered at a single community and each
politically independent. Such a model would fit much of the
archaeological evidence, and probably represents the arrangement
that existed during a large part of Maya history. But by Late Classic times, there is some reason to wonder whether larger units—
regional states including a number of ceremonial centers—had
not come into existence. Some sites like Tikal, Yaxchilan,
Palenque, and Copan grew to immense size in the Late Classic
and became much larger than most other centers. Tikal, for
example, had several times as many structures as Uaxactun, only
11 miles away. It is difficult to imagine that Tikal could not
have easily conquered or otherwise controlled Uaxactun had it
been of a mind to do so. The scenes of military conquest are also
suggestive of units surpassing city-state size. Scenes of Maya
nobles captured by or offering submission to other lords seem,
as already noted, far too grandiose to suggest purely local
events and were probably an end result of warfare between
major centers. It seems likely that at least some of the occasions
of warfare and conquest must have led to the incorporation of
defeated centers into the political spheres of their conquerors.

Although for a long time I preferred the city-state model for
Maya political organization, I now have the feeling that by the
Late Classic period regional states were beginning to appear in
the Maya lowlands, centered at places like Tikal and Yaxchilan.
These states were probably built partly by outright conquest,
but it may also be that lesser powers voluntarily affiliated themselves as a matter of self-protection and self-interest. To really
prove whether such states existed, we shall probably have to
wait until specialists in hieroglyphic inscriptions can tell us
more about historical details that are certainly hidden within still
untranslated sections of the inscriptions.

Lengthy though this chapter has been, it barely scratches the
surface of the topics that should be considered in a discussion
of social and political organization, and the points about which
it is not even possible to hazard the rude guesses attempted
here are legion. Social and political organization will certainly
receive increased attention in future archaeological work, but
the difficulties to be faced in reaching such abstract topics
through concrete remains of material culture will demand great
sophistication in research design.

7. Religion and Intellectual Achievement

Part of the allure of the Maya lies in the fact that they produced the most intellectual of the New World civilizations. Given more than most peoples to contemplation about the world and their place in it, to concern with omens and the fates they portend, and to genuine scholarship in such fields as astronomy and mathematics, the Maya have captured the imagination of modern sophisticates in much the same fashion as have the ancient Greeks or Egyptians. The fascination of still-undeciphered secrets or of possible understandings of the world now lost in the bustle of modern technology has led both to scholarly interest and to flights of the wildest romanticism.

A great deal of what we know of Maya religion and world view comes from much later times than those that concern us in this book. Accounts of observers who knew the Maya in days shortly after the Spanish Conquest, prophecies that were part of Maya lore, and the few precious prehistoric Maya books that have been found combine to give us lively, if at times confused, accounts of Maya thought of the fourteenth and fifteenth centuries. But this was many centuries after the Classic period, and the Maya had by then undergone bad days and extensive contacts with Mexican peoples that had undeniably influenced their ideas. We must therefore use these accounts with caution and must seek continually to check them against archaeological evidence from Classic sites if we are to attempt a reconstruction of earlier philosophy and theology.

The most exciting sources of evidence about Maya scholarship are the native manuscripts (called codices) written by the Maya themselves in times before the Spanish Conquest. Three of these codices are now known, named, after the cities in which they now rest, the Dresden Codex, the Paris Codex, and the Madrid Codex. All are written on a sort of paper that was made from the bark of the wild fig tree and then covered with fine plaster to serve as the base for hieroglyphic writing and pictures done with native pigments. The paper was made in long strips, which were folded like a screen to give a series of pages that are read from left to right. The strip is then turned over and the obverse also is read left to right. The Maya are said to have had hundreds of such books when they were first encountered by the Spanish, but all except three have been destroyed or lost. The tantalizing hope remains that hidden somewhere in little-explored document collections from the fifteenth and sixteenth centuries or in forgotten family treasures there may still be more such manuscripts. Any who might be prompted to a quest by such a hope, however, should have fair warning that fake codices abound and are regularly offered for sale to unwary collectors. Maya books are said to have been buried with their priest-owners in the Conquest period; in occasional Classic period burials, elusive fragments of crumbling plaster, too frag-mentary and eroded to reveal their original nature, suggest that similar practices went back to far earlier times. Given the delicate nature of Maya paper and the climatic conditions of the Maya lowlands, however, it would take freaks of preserva-tion too great to believe for a Classic codex to have survived in readable form.

The Dresden Codex is the most interesting and best executed of the Maya codices. It is thought to have been written in the twelfth or thirteenth century, but portions of it seem to have been copied from a far earlier codex that may have included material dating as far back as the Classic period. Some of the contents of the Dresden Codex—such as tables predicting eclipses and tables on the cycle of the planet Venus—are highly scholarly and would have been of meaning only to trained astronomical experts. There is more directly applicable informa-tion as well, such as almanacs that predict what agricultural conditions will be during certain periods of time. Representations and texts concerning New Year's ceremonies are also included.

The Paris Codex is an 11-page fragment of what must once have been a longer document. It too, probably dates to the twelfth or thirteenth century, but, like the Dresden Codex, may include material copied from earlier manuscripts. One entire side is devoted to consideration of a series of 11 successive *katuns* (20-year periods). Pictures and texts seem to refer to the gods that dominated each *katun* and probably include in-formation of a prophetic-historical nature. Prophecy and history were intertwined in the Maya view, for events that happened in a given period of time were expected to be repeated when that period returned again. The second side of the codex, which is poorly preserved, seems to deal with divinatory almanacs.

The Madrid Codex, the longest of the Maya codices (56 pages), is generally agreed to be late and probably was not written until some time in the last century before the Spanish Conquest. It contains none of the scholarly information on astronomy or calendrics that is present in the other two codices, but is devoted instead to divination, giving the auguries for each of a series of daily activities, such as hunting and beekeeping, in terms of calendric periods. The Madrid Codex has been likened to the sort of manual that might be of practical use to a relatively unschooled parish priest in counseling his parishioners.

Good sources for information about the beliefs of the Maya in times not long after the Spanish Conquest include the writings of Bishop Landa, an early bishop of Merida in Yucatan who was an astute observer of Maya life, and the books of *Chilam Balam,* books written by Maya priests in colonial times who used the Spanish alphabet to record sacred themes in their Yucatec Maya language. The accounts of ethnographers who have studied the Maya in recent times provide further information, for most of the old gods survive in Maya villages, although now thoroughly blended with Christian ideas and practices (Figure 22). Putting information from all these sources together makes possible at least a tentative reconstruction of what the ancient Maya may have believed about the world around them and the supernatural forces that directed it.

The Maya conceived of a universe in which the heavens were divided into 13 compartments arranged into 7 levels. Each compartment was ruled by a god. In similar fashion, the underworld had 9 divisions, each ruled by its own god. At the 4 edges of the earth were gods to help sustain the heavens, and each of the points of the compass was associated with a sacred tree and a special color. There also seems to have been a sacred tree at the earth's center, which may be the so-called Tree of Life pictured occasionally in Maya art as a source of good and abundance.

Modern Maya peoples in several regions still recount myths of the creation of men, which, since they share many common features, are probably of great antiquity. Almost all of these myths hold that the gods have created the world several times, but each time they have destroyed it because they have been dissatisfied with their own handicraft. The present world is the third, fourth, or fifth creation, depending upon which version of the story is being told. Implicit in the thought that the gods have destroyed previous creations is the possibility that our own world may meet a similar fate. Maintaining the favor of the gods thus becomes not simply a pious duty, but the key to existence itself.

Figure 22

Modern Maya Ceremony. *The Maya Indians of today still engage in a life rich in ceremonialism that has become a blend of Catholicism and far older native practices. Here, a group of Indians from Chiapas, Mexico, celebrate a fiesta with a procession and fireworks. (Arizona State Museum, University of Arizona, William Holland Collection.)*

To the Maya, the world abounded in supernatural beings and forces, so vast in number that it is almost impossible to sort them out into a system that seems coherent to a Western observer. Since the information available to us about Maya gods comes from a variety of different areas and time periods, and since it seems likely that in each time and place individual gods probably had a series of different guises, each guise differently portrayed, the confusion in the minds of the Maya worshipper was probably far less than that created in our minds by the multiplicity of fragmentary information. J. Eric Thompson, a foremost authority on ancient Maya religion, has pointed out several features of Maya gods that do much to add to the complexity of the Maya pantheon. In the first place, most gods, and perhaps all of them, appeared in four forms, which were associated with the world directions. Second, gods were dualistic in that they had both benevolent and malevolent aspects. Finally, gods tended to have aspects that were associated with diametrically opposed groups; the sun god, for example, was primarily associated with gods of the day, but since he also traveled through the underworld on his daily journey he was, also, in one of his forms, ranked among the gods of the night.

Only a few of the Maya gods can be mentioned in detail. *Itzamna* certainly deserves the first place in the discussion, since he appears to have been a particularly important god of the Classic period and at some times and places in Maya history became so all-pervasive that he took on aspects and functions of almost all other deities. In form and representation, *Itzamna* had reptilian features, combining elements of the crocodile, lizard, and snake or taking the form of the Classic period Celestial Monster. He was associated with both the earth and the sky, which the Maya seem to have viewed as part of an inseparable union. He was thought to send the life-giving rains and thus to be representative of fertility and abundance. In some accounts he appears as the creator of the world and of mankind.

The sun, *Ah Kin*, and the moon, *Ix Chel*, were gods to the Maya, although their cult seems to have faded to relative obscurity in later times after having enjoyed considerably more importance during the Classic period. They were sometimes viewed as man and wife and credited in legends with the invention of sexual intercourse. The fidelity of the moon, *Ix Chel*, was open to serious question, however; in addition to being the patroness of procreation and childbirth, she was also looked upon as the patroness of sexual license. *Ah Kin*, most frequently represented as an old man, was associated with drought and bad weather and was attended to more in order to avoid his wrath than to seek his benefits.

Beloved to the Maya peasant were the *Chacs*, thought to be the givers of rain. The *Chacs* are many, although in some contexts there is one principal *Chac* or sometimes four major *Chacs* associated with the world directions. Generally conceived in human form as old men with long beards, in the codices or older sculptures *Chacs* have some features relating them to the serpent. Frogs, particularly the remarkable *Uo* frog who emerges from his deeply buried hiding place only on the rainiest days of the year, are assistants to the *Chacs*, as is the tortoise.

Reverenced as a further expression of the Maya's interest in agricultural abundance is a Maize God, pictured invariably as a handsome young man. The planet Venus was also a god, as were other celestial phenomena. In addition, there were numerous gods associated with the Maya calendar; each day,

Figure 23

A Boatload of Maya Gods. *This scene, from a set of carved bones recovered from Burial 116 at Tikal, shows what are probably a series of Maya gods. The informality of the depiction is a strong contrast with the very stylized portraits of deities that are carved in stone. (The University Museum, University of Pennsylvania.)*

for example, had its own god. Spirits haunted natural phenomena, and the world of both living and inanimate things was peopled with a host of supernatural powers.

The fact that most Maya gods had animal attributes should by this time be obvious (Figure 23). Some gods seem to appear only in animal form. The jaguar, for instance, was immensely important to the Classic Maya and seems to have been a god. But to think of the Maya as worshiping animals may be quite inappropriate; the animal attributes may simply have been symbolic of qualities of divine beings, who were conceptualized in a quite different fashion. It may, for instance, be no more accurate to say that the Maya had a Jaguar God than to say simply because the Holy Spirit is represented as a dove in Christian art that some Christians worship a Dove God.

The role of religion among the Classic Maya is stressed in so many contexts throughout this book that there seems little need at this point to enlarge upon the magnitude of Classic investment in structures devoted to worship or the importance of priestly roles in the status system of the Maya. There is every reason to believe that the Maya went through an elaborate cycle of ceremonies set by one or the other of their calendars, and that particularly important events such as the beginning of a new year or the transitions marking even longer calendric periods were celebrated by many days of joyful activities. There

is also indication that key times in the agricultural cycle such as planting, arrival of the spring rains, and harvest were occasions for propitiation or thanks to the gods. The earth, the rains, and growing things of nature were treated with a loving respect and reverence long lost in our technological society (at least until the recent stirrings of renewed feelings about our place in nature). Before felling a tree or embarking on a hunting expedition, the Maya peasant of present-day Yucatan makes an offering to the gods and apologizes for the damage he is about to do, pointing out that his actions are necessary for survival and not done for selfish gain.

It is probably only consistent with the feeling of the Maya that they were an integral part of nature, that they should have seen their lives as influenced by a series of natural and supernatural forces. Fate loomed large to the Maya and they saw historical events as following natural courses that were foreordained from the beginnings of creation. But the fates were not whimsical—rather, they followed set patterns that could be known and used by men to take advantage of the forces of good and to minimize the effect of days of ill fortune.

This concept of the world was intimately related to Maya concern with divination, omens, and calendrics. As in astrology of today, the forces acting at any given time were complex and needed careful interpretation and study. The kinds of almanacs represented in the Maya codices that interpreted the luck or danger associated with a whole series of different activities according to the ruling gods of the day were much in keeping with the wish to understand the auguries of the time before beginning an action. It seems likely that during Classic times a whole corps of priest-specialists was kept busy in helping to decide the most favorable days for undertaking important ventures such as the Maya form of baptism, marriage, or building a house.

The Maya felt that history was cyclical and that the fate of one period of time would return when that period was once again in force. This cyclical view of history was particularly applied to the cycle of 13 20-year *katuns,* and there were long lists of *katun* prophecies specifying the nature of each of the 13 *katuns.* These prophetic statements incorporated examples of events that had happened in earlier times, a fact that makes them potentially useful historical documents; but the failure to distinguish in which of earlier periods a specific event occurred causes major problems in interpretation. An example of the fatalistic attitude of the Maya toward history comes from the story of the first attempts to subjugate and missionize the Itza, the last Maya kingdom with which the Spanish came in contact. When, in the late seventeenth century, missionaries came to the Itza at their capital of Tayasal in the heart of the Peten and asked them to accept the Christian God and the governance of the Spanish, they were told that the Itza could not do so then, but that if the missionaries would return in two years they would then be in the *Katun 8 Ahau.* Since *Katun 8 Ahau* was traditionally a period of major change in leadership and political matters, the Itza promised to submit to the Spanish at that time.

Sacrifices and offerings were a key part of Maya religious ritual. Today, food and drink, liquor, and other products of the field and forest are offered to the gods on ceremonial occasions (Figure 24). In Classic sites, remains of offerings abound in burials, under stelae, or beneath the floors of buildings; they often include rows of vessels, sometimes containing the dusty residues of what must have been perishable material. Shell, coral, sponges, and other products of the sea are abundant in offerings and suggest a Classic period emphasis upon water that must relate to concern with rainfall and agricultural abundance. The Classic Maya did not eschew human sacrifice, but they did not give it the emphasis it received in the Postclassic period. Self-sacrifice through bloodletting, however, was very common at the time of the Spanish Conquest, and several scenes on Classic sculpture seem to include rites of bloodletting. Either cactus spines or the sharp spine from the tail of the stingray were used in the Conquest period for bloodletting, and the existence of stingray spines in great frequency in Classic burials and offerings gives further evidence of autosacrificial practices.

A key role in ceremonialism among Maya Indians of today is played by processions that wind their way past a series of sacred stations, observing each one with prayers and offerings.

Although today natural features such as springs and caves are included with the church as holy places, one can easily imagine the Classic Maya honoring all their sacred locations with ceremonial construction. It is not unlikely that the causeways that are found within major Maya sites may have been constructed primarily to enhance the pomp and ease of much more luxuriant prehistoric processions. At the larger sites, the size of both causeways and open spaces such as plazas is such that thousands of people could have participated or observed without being crowded.

In summary, the religious practices of the Maya show great stability over a long period of time. Ceremonialism of the Classic period was of vastly larger scale than that of the present and

Figure 24

Modern Maya Offering. *Prayers and offerings continue to be an important part of Maya ceremonial life. Here, a sacred shrine in a cave in the highlands of Chiapas, Mexico, offers power to those who approach its patron gods. (Arizona State Museum, University of Arizona, William Holland Collection.)*

involved specialists in priestly matters who have long since passed from existence. But where archaeological evidence gives us hints of Classic ideas, the gods, beliefs, and observances are not fundamentally different from things that are well attested in colonial times and continue to persevere until the present.

A discussion of religion among the Classic Maya leads inexorably to a consideration of intellectual prowess, for Maya achievements in astronomy, calendrics, and mathematics were most vividly and triumphantly demonstrated in contexts that are clearly ceremonial.

The place to begin a consideration of Maya intellectual achievements is with the system of hieroglyphic writing. This was the only true writing system ever developed in the New World; the Incas had no more than a system of record keeping on knotted strings, and the Aztecs and other people of central Mexico had a pictographic script without true phonetic meaning. The Maya system was much more flexible and consequently more fully developed. Unfortunately, despite several generations of intensive effort, the Maya script remains untranslated. A goodly number of glyphs have been interpreted, to the extent that their meanings are generally agreed upon and the meanings can be used to elucidate the content of some passages. The work on calendrical and numerical glyphs has been particularly successful, and most of such passages can be "read" with ease. Interpretation of other kinds of accounts is much more fragmentary; although names, emblem glyphs of a number of sites, and some glyphs for historical events such as birth and death can now be interpreted, large sections of text that must contain fascinating material are completely uninterpretable.

By this time, my distinction between *interpreting* and *reading* hieroglyphs must have become hopelessly obscure, so I will attempt to clarify it. We know that a particular glyph used in certain contexts stands for "captor of." In other words, we can *interpret* what it *means*. At the same time, we do not know what Maya word or sounds it stands for; in fact, we are not even sure what language is represented by the inscriptions. Consequently we cannot *read* the "captor of" glyph; that is, we cannot pronounce it in Maya. Furthermore, if the glyph is encountered in a context where it clearly does not mean "captor of," we have no clue to what its meaning may be in this new context. It is as if we had learned that in English the letters e-a-r standing alone refer to the familiar piece of auditory apparatus attached to the head. This does not help us at all in figuring out the words "earn" or "early," where the three letters make no reference to ears or to hearing—nor could we safely translate even the word "hear" itself, where the occurrence of the same three letters and similarity of meaning (and even of pronunciation) is merely a coincidence.

To discuss the possibility of translating an unknown script demands an initial consideration of the kind of writing involved. There are several different ways of transposing language to written form. The simplest, so simple that it does not deserve the title of true writing, is pictographic. It involves the use of pictures of things to stand for the things themselves and has the limitation that only concrete, depictable objects can be represented. Most of the prehistoric scripts from central Mexico consisted of little more than picture writing.

More advanced systems of representation use abstract symbols to represent things, and symbols can be employed in several different ways. Some scripts are ideographic, with each symbol standing for an entire idea. Ideographic writing systems are cumbersome because they require an immensely large number of different signs to stand for all the things and ideas that a communication system must refer to. They are, however, not dependent on a particular language, since anyone familiar with what ideas the signs represent can read the material in his own language. Another possibility is to use a phonetic system, in which each symbol stands for a sound used in the language. The symbols can then be combined (as sounds are) to make words. Phonetic languages can be either alphabetic, using symbols for individual sounds as we do in English, or syllabic, using symbols that stand for consonant-vowel combinations. Phonetic writing systems are economical in the number of symbols needed, but they are language dependent and cannot be read without knowing the language that they represent. There is no law that requires writing systems to be consistent, however, and any particular system may combine several (or even all) of the principles just described.

The opinion currently favored is that the Maya writing system was some sort of hybrid. It contains far too many separate glyphs to be alphabetic and even too many for a completely syllabic system. On the other hand, there are not nearly enough glyphs for an ideographic system. It looks, then, as if Maya writing combines both syllabic and ideographic elements, with the former probably predominating.

What is the chance that Maya glyphs will some day be translated? Linguistic experts feel that if there are strong syllabic components, chances are very good, although the amount of time and effort needed will be high. The first task in breaking a syllabic script is to reconstruct the Maya language as it would have been a thousand years ago. Languages change through time, and anyone who has struggled with Chaucer or Beowulf in the original can testify that the changes may be quite drastic. Since there is no record available that gives us information about the Maya language as it was spoken in A.D. 500, the language must be reconstructed by comparing the series of Maya languages that exist today. Since linguistic change follows regular patterns, the task is quite possible, and the techniques are already well known. Given the form of a Classic Maya language, computers could be used in a series of complex procedures to derive the syllabic values of glyphs—again, the process is lengthy and difficult but not impossible. As the number of correct interpretations of glyphs grows, the ease of translating others increases, and any glyphs that have nonsyllabic meaning will also become easier to interpret.

If the job of translating Maya hieroglyphs is accomplished, what will we learn about the Maya? Certainly we can count on adding considerable new information about Maya history and about religious beliefs and practices, since this would seem to be the kind of material most likely to be dealt with in still untranslated passages. We may also learn something about social and economic organization, if titles of people within the administrative structure of Maya society appear with regularity in the texts. On the other hand, we do not have any real economic documents; if there were things like accounts or tax roles in the Classic sculptures, they would already be obvious from the associated mathematics. It would be interesting to know whether the Maya used their script in any way for economic matters. If they did not, they were the only literate people in the history of the world who managed to keep writing out of the hands of the bill collector and the tax man. It is not likely, however, that even the Maya were so sophisticated, and extensive archives of records on paper could easily have existed and decayed away without leaving the faintest archaeological trace.

All the other Maya intellectual accomplishments to be discussed here depend upon skill and sophistication in mathematics. At some time before A.D. 300, someone in Mesoamerica invented a system of positional notation for counting. Such a system, consisting of a series of "places" for units of continually increasing magnitude (like our own series of ones, tens, hundreds, etc.) greatly facilitates dealing with large numbers and increases the ease of computation. Positional notation depends upon grasping the highly abstract notion of a zero quantity and upon having a symbol for zero. Until discovery of the Maya system, it was thought that positional notation and the concept of zero had been invented only once in human history—by the Hindus in the eighth century, from which source it spread to Europe where it was not adopted until the fifteenth century. It is now evident that in this fundamental mathematical advance, the Western world ran a bad last and that the credit for first discovery goes to some unknown mathematical genius in the New World. Since the concept must have been invented some time before we see the first record of it—the first record is in very complex calendrical notations, which could not have been developed without previous knowledge of the zero concept—it is not clear which area of Mesoamerica should get credit for the invention. Whether or not the Maya were the actual inventors, however, they were certainly the ones who used the results most effectively.

The Western world does not fare much better in comparison with the Maya in terms of calendrical precision. The Maya were fascinated by the stately procession of days and years marching from the past into the unknown future, and they developed an incredible sophistication in dealing with temporal and astronomical cycles. Their fascination was such that they were not satisfied with a single functioning calendar. Instead, they used a series of different cycles, all running at the same time and interweaving in incredibly complex fashions. One of these calendars consisted of 260 days formed by combining the numbers from 1 to 13 with 20 day names. The 260-day calendar had deep religious significance. Each of the 20 named days was a god, and the god had a set augury, portending either good or evil luck. However, the combination with each of the 13 numbers changed the portent to some degree, so that each of the 260 days had a slightly different meaning.

The origin of the 260-day cycle is obscure. It is widespread in Mesoamerica and must be very ancient, so it remains unclear whether the Maya should receive credit for its invention. What gave rise to the idea of a 260-day cycle is also quite uncertain, for it corresponds to no prominent celestial phenomenon. Such diverse opinions as that it may relate to the length of the cycle of human pregnancy or to the length of time needed to grow a crop of maize have been raised. In effect, a guessing game is in operation, and almost anything that lasts about 260 days can be suggested. Since there is no obvious way to check the correctness of any suggestion, the game may well continue interminably.

The Maya also had a calendar that made a 365-day "year,"

a figure close to the true length of the tropical year. The 365-day year was broken down into 18 months of 20 days each, followed by a special period of 5 extremely unlucky days added to reach the proper total of 365. Each month was associated with a god and had divinatory significance, although less than that for the days of the 260-day cycle. The five final days of the year were met with great dismay by the Maya, and any activity whatsoever was avoided as far as possible.

A period of 365 days, however, is actually about one-quarter day short of the true length of the solar year, so the Maya 365-day cycle slipped backward in relation to the seasons at the rate of about one full day each 4 years. The Maya knew with great accuracy the exact solar year, but rather than correcting their 365-day calendar by adding extra days at appropriate intervals (as in our own leap years) they chose to allow the slow rotation of the calendar around the seasons. Whenever they inscribed a date, however, they added a correction formula that indicated how many days away from the correct seasonal position the 365-day calendar was at that particular time. The correction formulae revealed an extremely accurate notion of solar phenomena. In fact, a correction formula introduced at the Lowland Maya site of Copan in the sixth century A.D. made the Maya year slightly more accurate than our present Gregorian year, which was not introduced as the standard calendar in Western civilization until 1582, nearly 1000 years later than the Copan correction.

Each day for the Maya was named for its position in both the 260-day and 365-day calendars. A day, for example, would be designated 4 *Kan* 2 *Pop*, indicating that at that particular time the 260-day cycle had reached 4 *Kan* while the 365-day cycle was at 2 *Pop*. As might well be imagined, the time at which both cycles reached their New Year's days together was an event of great significance. Such double New Year's days occurred only once each 52 years, and the 52-year period so created was known as the Calendar Round.

The Calendar Round does not give an exact date for a long series of events, however; a day 4 *Kan* 2 *Pop* is unique only for a particular 52-year cycle, and simply to give the day name does not distinguish it from other days 4 *Kan* 2 *Pop* that occurred in earlier cycles or will occur in later ones. To give exact dates for a long series, a calendar must have a fixed starting point, such as the birth of Christ in the Western calendar. The Maya recognized the need for such a fixed starting point and established it as a particular day 4 *Ahau* 8 *Cumhu* which would have fallen in the year 3113 B.C. in the Christian calendar under the correlation of Maya and Christian calendars accepted here. But even an overwhelming admiration for the Maya cannot prompt one to imagine this date as relating to a specific event actually remembered by the Maya; therefore it must refer to some mythical event, perhaps the day thought to be that of the creation of the present world.

Given this fixed starting point, it is only necessary to count how many days have elapsed to establish a fixed and unique date. The Maya could have done this in any of a number of ways. They might have used the number of elapsed 260-day or 365-day cycles or the number of elapsed Calendar Rounds (each of these plus any additional days since the completion of the last full cycle). With their passion for keeping calendrics complicated, however, the Maya used a completely different system to count elapsed days. This system was a 5-place notation in which the lowest place had as the unit 1 *kin* (1 day); the next unit was 1 *uinal* (20 days); the third unit was 1 *tun* (18 *uinals* or 360 days—note, however, that this unit, although it approximates a year, matches neither the solar year nor the Maya 365-day year); the fourth unit is 1 *katun* (20 *tuns*); and the fifth unit is 1 *baktun* (20 *katuns*). A Maya date, then, might read 9.16.6.0.5, which would mean that it was 9 *baktuns*, 16 *katuns*, 6 *tuns*, 0 *uinals*, and 5 *kins* after the starting date in 3113 B.C. This dating system, called the Long Count, was used only during the Maya Classic period, with the earliest recorded date— 8.12.14.8.15—occurring on Stela 29 at Tikal and the most recent—10.4.0.0.0—on a jadeite gorget from Quintana Roo in southern Mexico.

During the Postclassic period, the Maya used a shortened form of dating that was less exact and did not contain a full count of all days elapsed from the starting date of the calendar. The failure to carry the full Long Count through to the time at which it could be recorded by the Spaniards means that the exact correlation of the Maya Long Count and Christian calendars is a matter of some debate. All transpositions of Maya dates into our calendar quoted in this book follow the Goodman-Martínez-Thompson correlation of the two calendars, the most generally accepted correlation at the present time. Without going into remarkable details that would surely lose all readers except a few obsessed with calendars or mathematical games, little more can be said than that other possible correlations of the Maya and Christian calendars exist, but that the one used here is now accepted by the great majority of experts.

The calendrical precision just discussed would have been impossible without very detailed astronomical records. Maya astronomers did not confine their interests to the solar phenomena involved in calculating the length of the year, however; they had, in addition, very exact knowledge of the phases of the moon and the cycle of the planet Venus. Perhaps their most noteworthy accomplishment besides the calendar was the derivation of formulae to predict the days on which eclipses of the sun or the moon would take place. Although the Maya could not have developed the ability to say which of these eclipses would actually be visible in their area, they did know exactly when such eclipses were possible and undoubtedly used this information to tremendous advantage in impressing a populace who viewed eclipses as magical and extremely dangerous events.

It is remarkable that a people living in an area where the trees shut out the sky in most places and where cloud cover is heavy during many parts of the year should create such astronomical expertise. To develop their knowledge so fully the Maya must have had a corps of highly trained and specialized astronomers, a long and accurate record of observations, and a system of communication that kept observers from different sites in touch with each other's work. Records from inscriptions demonstrate that new astronomical niceties spread from one end of the Maya lowlands to the other within very short periods of time, and a stone carving from the site of Copan, a very innovative astronomical center, is generally thought to represent a conference of astronomical experts convened from major sites throughout the lowlands. The possible conference occurred at a time when Copan introduced an important new calendrical correlation that spread with lightning speed, appearing not long thereafter in the inscriptions of a series of widely scattered sites.

The Maya clearly demonstrate that although the scientific tradition of Western civilization is long and honorable, the West had by no means had a monopoly in scholarly achievement. In the first millenium of the Christian era, the natives of Mesoamerica, and particularly the Maya, were world leaders in a number of realms of scientific endeavor.

8. The Late Classic Period

The summary of the Early Classic period in Chapter 3 provides a picture of a successful society. In the Late Classic period, beginning in A.D. 600, Maya Classic culture intensified the trends of the Early Classic in a boom cycle that took it onward to spectacularly bigger and better things at an ever-accelerating pace. Looked at without knowledge of the end result, one would have to say that the Late Classic Maya were even more successful than their Early Classic progenitors. But rapid growth and expansion can be dangerous. An exploding population, an overheating economy, and a reckless investment in public works can eventually begin to run out of control, and by the time a realization of the situation dawns, no force on earth can brake the system short of the disaster that impends. Such seems to have been the case with the Late Classic Maya, for less than three centuries ahead they faced a disaster that has few parallels in human history. It behooves us to look carefully at the fall of the Maya and the events that preceded it, for a computer simulation of the present world system recently summarized in book form in *The Limits to Growth*[1] suggests that we ourselves stand at the brink of one of those cycles of uncontrolled acceleration such as may have ended the career of Maya civilization.

The most obvious feature of the pattern of Late Classic Maya expansion is the growth in population. The number of housemounds at Tikal more than doubled between the Early Classic and the height of the Late Classic crowding, in A.D. 750. Everywhere a shovel is put in the ground near occupied areas of Tikal it reaps a reward of Late Classic potsherds, a mute testimonial of long-vanished activity. The population increase is even more striking, however, in some of the regions away from the central Peten. Sites on both the Pasion and Usumacinta rivers seem to have had very sparse Early Classic populations. People were

---

[1] Donella H. Meadows et al., *The Limits to Growth: A Report for the Club of Rome's Project on the Predicament of Mankind* (New York: Universe, 1972).

certainly there, for stelae were erected at Altar de Sacrificios on the Pasion and at Piedras Negras on the Usumacinta in the heart of the Early Classic, but excavation projects at the same sites have had to search frantically for enough Early Classic pottery to complete the ceramic sequences. The Late Classic is quite a different story; all the river sites give evidence of increasingly heavy populations, until they, like Tikal, are loaded with Late Classic remains. Although there are data from far too few sites to attempt exact estimates of population growth for the entire Maya lowlands, it requires few mental gymnastics to hazard a guess that Late Classic population expansion was phenomenal throughout the area.

The population explosion was mirrored by a corresponding increase in monumental architecture. At Tikal, for example, the Early Classic center composed of a fully developed North Acropolis facing a large open area was changed by the construction of Temples 1 and 2 to define the Great Plaza. Both over 150 feet tall, these great temples in themselves represent backbreaking undertakings, but they make up no more than a tiny fraction of Late Classic construction. Three other great temples, numbers 3, 4, and 5, were also constructed then. Temple 4, the largest single structure at Tikal, stands 212 feet in height and measures 200 feet on a side at the base of its pyramid. At each 20-year *katun* period during the Late Classic the Tikal Maya erected a new Twin Pyramid Complex, each consisting of two large four-stairwayed pyramids, a nine-doorway gallery structure, and an open-roofed enclosure for a carved stela and altar. In addition, the Central Acropolis, four acres of solid palaces and plazas at the south edge of the Great Plaza, is almost entirely of Late Classic date, as are palace groups F, G, and H, all of them larger than any single complex in the Central Acropolis. The list of other masonry structures built at Tikal during the Late Classic would run to dozens, and many of these structures rivaled the size of the famous buildings in the site center. The total bulk of Late Classic construction is breathtaking. Tikal must have been a beehive of activity, with huge crews of laborers almost continually engaged (except perhaps during critical parts of the farming season) in quarrying and shaping limestone blocks, burning lime for plaster, amassing quantities of refuse for pyramid fill, and the actual operations of building. Millions of man-hours of labor are represented, both of unskilled crews and of highly trained masons, sculptors, architects, and administrators. Although the large population was of value as a labor pool, the strain on food and other resources would not have been mitigated by the fact that there was work available in plenty.

But Tikal was not a special case; excavation and architectural survey in all parts of the Maya lowlands suggest the same kind of feverish Late Classic activity. It is almost as though sites everywhere were in a heated race to reach the millenium in service to their gods and in contributing to the ease and elegance of their elite classes. Certainly no hint of impending doom seems to have tempered the grandiose plans of Maya priest and architect.

In pottery, too, the Late Classic shows an increase in "action." The Early Classic had been a period of three centuries during which there was almost no change in pottery style. Archaeologists all over the Maya lowlands, who depend on stylistic change in ceramics to provide a vital yardstick for dating, have cursed and sweated over the difficulties of making temporal subdivisions in the intractable Early Classic material. For a long while we all blamed ourselves for our difficulties or, in more confident moments, blamed the kinds of samples we had found. It now looks as though we can blame the Early Classic Maya, who seem to have been quite satisfied with their pottery and not the least bit interested in changing it. Late Classic ceramics pose no such problems. Changes are clear and rapid and suggest an air of experimentation and interest in trying new things. To draw broader conclusions from changes in ceramics involves guesswork of the crudest sort, but I am tempted to guess that the ceramic change relates to an increase in the resources that consumers had available for local specialized products and consequent innovation among specialists to stimulate consumer demands. Anyone who has watched the monthly parade of soaps with new ingredients and revolutionary breakthroughs in hair sprays is familiar with this type of cycle. Again, the specter of a successful, expanding, and highly competitive economy seems to loom before us.

There are also signs of change in the social status system of the Maya between the Early Classic and the Late Classic. William L. Rathje has recently completed an insightful analysis of offerings that accompanied Maya burials. His data show that who was buried where with what changed through time in ways that permit inferences about status. Particularly, burials made in small housemound groups differed from those made in palaces and temples located within ceremonial precincts. Not unexpectedly, offerings placed with burials in the ceremonial precincts (Figure 25) were usually richer than offerings in housemound burials. But the kinds of people buried in temples and palaces changed during the Classic period. In the earlier parts of the Classic, only mature adult males were buried in these locations (except for one burial of an infant who may have been the victim of a ceremonial sacrifice). By the end of the Classic, palace-temple burials included both males and females and individuals of all ages from infant to elderly. Even some of the very young individuals buried in the ceremonial precincts had rich burial offerings, suggesting that wealth and status had already accrued to them. It seems as though ceremonial center burial changed during the Classic period from a privilege reserved for mature males to a right available to entire families.

Housemound burials showed different patterns. In the earlier parts of the Classic period, fewer mature adults were buried in housemounds than would have been expected, but by the end of the Classic, housemound burials included a full complement of people of all ages. The earlier housemound burials also demonstrated an interesting pattern of offerings; a number of

Figure 25

Burial 116, Tikal. *Burial 116, found deeply hidden within the pyramid under Temple 1, was one of the richest burials encountered at Tikal. Of Late Classic date, the burial contained the skeleton of an adult male (visible at the center of the photograph) who may have been during his lifetime the high priest of Temple 1. He was surrounded by an abundance of goods, among which the ceramic vessels and seashells are visible in the photograph. On his chest were dozens of immense jade beads that once must have been part of necklaces. (The University Museum, University of Pennsylvania.)*

young adult burials had unexpectedly rich grave goods, richer than the offerings accompanying any other age group. By the end of the Classic, housemound burials uniformly had very poor offerings, regardless of age and sex.

What do these data tell us about the structure of Classic Maya society? Rathje notes that the earlier pattern of fairly rich young adults buried in housemounds and mature adults split between poor burials in housemounds and rich burials in ceremonial centers matches what would be expected in a society where wealth and social position were gained by an individual's effort during his lifetime. Younger people, living in housemound groups, would be working at accumulating wealth; if they chanced to die while still young, they would be buried in house-mounds with the possessions they had amassed, which in some cases might have been considerable. Among those who lived to maturity, some would succeed in their efforts to gain the possessions and status necessary to be admitted to ceremonial center activities and would eventually receive honored (and rich) burial in the center. Those who failed to make it socially would live out their lives in relative poverty and would be buried as poor adults in housemound groups.

Rathje notes that the later burial patterns certainly would not fit the society just described, but they do match what would be expected from a quite different social arrangement. A key factor in these later burials is that ceremonial centers, like house-mounds, contain burials with a full complement of males and females, young and old. It seems as though whole families lived in (or at least participated in the benefits of) the ceremonial center. Since even some children, far too young to have amassed wealth through their own efforts, were buried with rich offerings, wealth must have been passed on in family lines. Families of upper-class status, transmitting wealth and social position through inheritance, would constitute an aristocracy. The growth of such an aristocracy would make it increasingly difficult for lower-class individuals to gain wealth and would restrict the opportunity for achievement inferred from earlier burial patterns. In such a case, the general impoverishment of housemound burials would be an expectable result.

If Rathje's interpretations are correct, Maya social structure was changing between the Early Classic and Late Classic. Society in the Early Classic would have been more mobile, with opportunity for an individual to move up the social ladder by his own efforts, perhaps by way of mechanisms like participation in a *cargo* system. With time, social divisions became more rigid, and an emerging class of nobles increasingly tended to keep their hands on wealth and prestige passed down along family lines.

There are also architectural clues to changes in emphasis in Maya society. As noted in Chapter 3, the temple was far and away the dominant feature in Early Classic construction. In the Late Classic, the palace began to take on more and more importance. There was not actually any decrease in temple construction; in fact, more temples were probably built in the Late Classic than in the Early Classic. But with the burst of Late Classic architectural fervor, an ever-increasing *proportion* of energy and labor turned to palaces, which blossomed in available open spaces and eventually crept up to surround, or even overwhelm, what had earlier been purely ceremonial precincts. A striking case of this process was revealed when the Carnegie Institution excavated Structure A-V at the site of Uaxactun. The structure began its history in Early Classic times as a complex of three small temples seated on a low platform and completely open to view from one side (Figure 26). Not long thereafter three shrines were built along the open side of the platform, screening the area from view but not changing its religious character (Figure 27). A new secular note was added next as a large palace

Figure 26

Uaxactun, Structure A-V, Stage 1. *In this and the following architectural reconstructions by Tatiana Proskouriakoff, one can follow the changes in Structure A-V as it was rebuilt during Early and then Late Classic times. This first stage is completely ceremonial in character, for all three structures are temples. (The Peabody Museum, Harvard University.)*

Figure 27

Uaxactun, Structure A-V, Stage 4. *The three front shrines erected
by this stage supplied greater privacy for ceremonies but did not
change the ceremonial nature of Structure A-V. (The Peabody
Museum, Harvard University.)*

was constructed in front of the shrines. Then one of the temples
was torn down and replaced by a very imposing palace (Figure
28); another temple soon met the same fate. By the time modi-
fication of the complex ceased in the Late Classic period, palace-
type buildings had covered the platform like a cancerous
growth, so completely enveloping the one temple that remained
that only the tip of its roof comb peeked out from above the
maze of palaces (Figure 29). Obviously, the entire function of
the group had drastically changed.

We must now turn to the long-deferred question of the use
of the structures we call palaces. First, it is obvious that palaces
were designed for different uses than temples. Their basic
arrangement of long series of rooms provides much more interior
space than temples, and the broad spacious stairways of palaces,
often stretching the entire length of the building, suggest that
they were designed for easy and convenient access. Palaces also
show a number of distinctive features lacking in temples.
Benches are commonplace, sometimes so large that they take
up most of the space in a room. Thrones with masonry armrests

occur with some frequency, usually placed just inside doorways that command majestic views of open courtyards. In the wall in each side of palace doorways there are holes lined with ceramic inserts, which are conjectured to be curtain holders by which it would be possible to hang textiles to close the door against prying eyes. Kitchen facilities, however, are absent; there are neither hearths nor walls covered with the soot of cooking fires. This need not rule out domestic function, however, since even today the Maya traditionally build kitchens as separate rooms—frequently crude lean-to shelters attached to the sides of houses.

None of this information provides conclusive proof of function, so we must rely upon the logic of inference until someone can think of definitive tests that can be applied to choose between alternative uses. One obvious possibility, as implied by the name given the structures, is that palaces were the homes of members of the Maya elite. Some archaeologists protest that palace rooms are too dark and damp to have been livable. Much of the present aura of the rooms, however, can be attributed to

Figure 28

Uaxactun, Structure A-V, Stage 6. *The addition of a large palace building at the back of the group and probably an administrative building at the front have added secular features to the structure. (The Peabody Museum, Harvard University.)*

Figure 29

Uaxactun, Structure A-V, Stage 8. *By this final stage of Structure A-V, almost all of the buildings are secular in character and only one small temple remains. (The Peabody Museum, Harvard University.)*

the dense surrounding vegetation, which shuts out light and impedes air circulation. In prehistoric times, with most of the vegetation removed and the sun gleaming from plastered courtyards, palaces would have been far from dark and damp. In fact, they probably provided cool and welcome respite from the heat and glare of cleared open spaces.

Not to be overlooked either are the lengths to which people will go to attain that most intangible and luxurious of commodities—prestige. Pinching shoes, eye-bulging girdles, cars that compress the human body into spaces that would be prohibited for animal transport, cocktail parties that strain believable levels of boredom—the list of things endured for prestige in our own society is almost endless. Whatever the use of Maya palaces, they obviously carried enormous prestige, and that fact by itself is probably enough to overweigh any inconvenience or unpleasantness they may have had. Finally, many features found in palaces would be useful in residential quarters. Doorways closed by curtains suggest domestic privacy. Benches could have been used for sleeping. In all, I am convinced that at least some palace rooms were living quarters and that those who lived there were in the upper levels of Maya society.

Another possibility is that palaces served administrative functions as places of contact between elite officials and other persons. Contacts could have ranged from formal occasions of state—royal audiences for local people or for visiting dignitaries —to the daily bureaucratic routine of clerks and tax collectors. Maya painting and carving frequently depict rulers seated upon thrones being approached by visitors or suppliants (Figure 30). One can easily imagine stately processions approaching the throne rooms of palaces with all the pomp and circumstance of medieval court occasions. On a less grand level, Maya society must have had its full share of petty bureaucrats. Some palace rooms could well have housed long tables at which the public could meet with bureaucratic underlings to make payments, seek information, or do any of the myriad other duties that complex societies demand of their citizens. I find no contradiction in believing that Maya palaces served both residential and administrative functions; such multipurpose use would fit well with the large numbers of palaces that existed by the end of the Late Classic as well as with the great variation they show in size, room arrangement, and internal features.

Figure 30

Throne Scene. *This illustration, taken from a painted vessel found in Tikal Burial 116, shows a scene common in Maya art—a ruler receiving homage from his subjects. From the context in an important burial, it seems likely that the individual on the throne is the same individual buried in the tomb. (The University Museum, University of Pennsylvania.)*

The increasing investment in palace structures during the Late Classic points to a growth in the importance of administrators
and nobles. No longer were the gods almost the sole beneficiaries of architectural activity as they had been in the Early Classic. Gods moved over on their pedestal to make room for humans, and humans proved more adept than the gods at manipulating the system to their benefit. Rising secularity, or the emphasis of the human as well as the divine, is a trend that can be seen in a number of early civilizations. It usually gave rise to the emergence of the institution of kingship and the dominance of society by an extremely powerful individual who—aided by his establishment of bureaucrats and military men, all personally loyal to the king himself rather than to the gods—ran society as his personal possession. Maya society in the Peten did not survive long enough for the naked force of kingship to triumph completely over the earlier religious emphasis, but the trend in that direction seems to have been set by Late Classic developments.

Concomitant with the secularization of Late Classic Maya society was a rise in military activity. For a long time there was a tendency among archaeologists to underplay the violent aspects of Maya culture. In some of the more extreme statements, the Maya sound like prehistoric pacifists bedecked in floral garlands and meditating upon no topic not touched with peace and sweetness. Part of this emphasis on Maya nonviolence results from a contrast between the Maya and later Mesoamerican peoples who did, indeed, carry violence to extremes that would excite pangs of envy even among the current generation of Hollywood directors. The Aztecs claim to have sacrificed 20,000 victims at the dedication of their major temple and fought wars for sheer sport when they could not find political or economic reasons for doing so. By comparison, the Maya were certainly a gentle folk. But their gentleness was not without blemish, for ample evidence of both war and human sacrifice awaits any objective evaluation of the archaeological and pictographic record they have left for us.

Prisoners are the most common theme indicative of warfare among the Maya (Figure 31). Bound, often prostrate, persons appear with frequency in sculpture as far back in time as the earliest known carvings. That the bound individuals are notable persons rather than common criminals or social deviants is demonstrated by the fact that many wear symbols of high office. In the Late Classic, scenes of actual fighting appear with increasing frequency. Usually these scenes are carved in stone and consist of almost symbolic representations of a ruler subduing

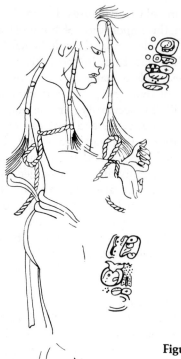

Figure 31

Bound Prisoner. *One of the masterpieces of Maya art, this representation of a prisoner is taken
from a carved bone found in Tikal
Burial 116. (The University Museum, University of Pennsylvania.)*

an opponent. In the famous Late Classic murals at the site of
Bonampak, the painted format provides the opportunity for
a full-scale battle scene in which a squadron of gaudily garbed
warriors attacks an opposing force that seems to have been
surprised, since none of them have donned uniforms or taken
up weapons. The denouement of the battle scene appears in
another mural panel (Figure 32) in which the prisoners, some of
them already dead or dying, plead for mercy at the feet of the
jaguar-skin-clad leader of the military expedition. Although warfare seems to have occurred from at least the beginning of the
Early Classic, the frequency with which military exploits become
the subject of art distinctly increases in the Late Classic. Increasing population, competition for land and other desirable
resources, and increasingly powerful secular lords are a lethal

combination that has led more than one society along the path
to disaster. Whether internal warfare had increased enough to
be a major problem for the Late Classic Maya is not clear, but
their circumstances certainly seem to have been apt for increasingly bitter competition.

There were few powers in the rest of Mesoamerica that could
trouble the Maya during most of the Late Classic period. Mighty
Teotihuacan had fallen even before the beginning of the Late
Classic, and its empire or domain had shaken off the mantle of
unification. A power vacuum and period of political confusion
seem to have resulted, in which several sites that had been
under the influence of Teotihuacan became important within
their own regions and probably contended with each other for
wider spheres of power. None of them was really successful,
however, and it was well after the fall of the Maya before

Figure 32

Judgment of Prisoners in Bonampak Murals. *This scene, portraying
the aftermath of a battle, shows the prisoners from the battle ar-
raigned before a leader in jaguar skins. Since some of the prisoners
seem to be already dead, the fate of captured warriors among the
Classic Maya seems to have been unfortunate. (The Peabody Museum, Harvard University.)*

anyone again created a sphere of influence that embraced all
Mesoamerica. Thus, throughout much of the Late Classic the
Maya do not seem to have faced serious threats from outside
their borders. Whether such threats arose just before the Maya
collapse, and may even have precipitated it, is a matter of debate
to be discussed in the chapter about the fall of Classic Maya
civilization.

In summary, *bigger and better* was the theme of the Late
Classic period of Maya history. Population growth, economic
expansion, and unparalleled activity in construction and stone
carving set the pace in a Maya boom time that must have
seemed, while it was in progress, to be solid evidence of the
success of the Maya experiment in rain forest civilization. That
Maya society would have to change under the impetus of
growth was inevitable. Profits were to be made, and the accumulation of the profits in the hands of an increasingly wealthy
elite who passed their resources on to their own descendants
was not a surprising result. That some of the wealth that remained after the gods had been thanked and placated by new
and larger temples should be turned to luxury for the elite and
the creation of bureaucracies to produce and handle still more
income was also expectable. But times were good for the non-
elite as well, and increased supplies of locally manufactured
consumer goods offered even the peasants a share of the economic boom. Imported goods may have become scarce at times
because the supply system had trouble handling demand from
an exploding population; bad crop years may have been hard
to handle for the same reason. But temporary concerns could be
easily forgotten in the midst of plenty. One wonders whether
there may have been prophets of doom who rose, perhaps to
be laughed to scorn, to question whether uncontrolled expansion was really good. If there were such prophets, history
has proved them correct, as we shall see in Chapter 9.

9. The Maya Collapse

Since the days of the nineteenth-century explorers, busy in the rain forest wilderness rediscovering the long-forgotten traces of Maya civilization, it has been obvious that some mysterious fate befell the Classic Maya. The ruined, overgrown state of the ancient centers revealed that for centuries they had housed no creatures more substantial than birds and spider monkeys. Documents from colonial times only added to the mystery. Cortés, the conqueror of Mexico, had passed across the heart of the Maya lowlands in 1525 and recounted his journey in a letter to the King of Spain. The missionaries and soldiers who led final pacification of the area just before the start of the eighteenth century also left accounts of their travels. All of these visitors had encountered the same vast expanse of silent rain forest that covers the area today, and the few native settlements they passed were small and impoverished. The local settlements failed to arouse even the lively imaginations of the Spanish, ready though they were to report cities of gold with teeming populations at the slightest provocation. The evidence all indicated that the Classic Maya had disappeared somewhere in the time-shrouded past and had left no modern descendants with even a faint touch of their glory and accomplishments.

The mystery deepened when the Maya calendar was deciphered and the history of carved dates emerged. At 9.18.0.0.0 of the Maya calendar (A.D. 790) no fewer than 19 different centers in the lowlands had erected dated monuments, the largest number ever to commemorate the ending of a 20-year *katun*. At 9.19.0.0.0 (A.D. 810), 12 centers, a still respectable number, dedicated stelae. But by 10.0.0.0.0 (A.D. 830) the number had dropped to 3 sites. Only 60 years later (10.3.0.0.0, or A.D. 889) the last stelae bearing full calendrical inscriptions in the Long Count dating system were carved, and with them an era had ended. These data suggested that the Maya collapse was as sudden as it was complete, for only a little over a century spanned the period from the very peak of the calendric cult to its final eclipse.

Striking though this information was, it still offered very incomplete evidence. All it really proved was that the Maya had stopped carving dates in stone rather suddenly in the ninth century and by the sixteenth century had abandoned their ancient centers and decreased greatly in population. There was no good reason to think that a decline in population and building activities might not have been a slow process that lasted for several centuries after carved dates were foresaken. Far more detailed archaeological work was needed to fit additional pieces into the puzzle.

The needed work has now been done, and the picture it reveals is stark indeed. Tikal can once more serve as an example, since we took special care at the site to investigate the period spanning the Maya collapse. The relevant time period is defined by two kinds of ceramics. One, called the Imix Ceramic Complex, lasted from A.D. 700 to A.D. 830. It was followed by the Eznab Ceramic Complex, which is dated between A.D. 830 and A.D. 900. Imix ceramics spanned the greatest century in Tikal's history. While the ceramics were in use, all five of the great temples at Tikal were built, six Twin Pyramid complexes were erected, and dozens of immense palaces took shape. Total population of the site displayed a similar peak, and more than 90 percent of Tikal housemounds were occupied during Imix times.

Eznab pottery is a direct outgrowth of Imix, and there can be no doubt that it followed immediately thereafter and was made by the descendants of the people who produced Imix vessels. But the contrast in achievements of the two groups could hardly be greater. After the great architectural enterprises of Imix, the best things the Eznab population could construct were a tiny platform in an outlying area of the site, a couple of benches placed inside palaces that had been built earlier, and patches on floors here and there. Not a single complete structure can be credited to Eznab builders.

The evidence about population density and location is even more astounding. Of several hundred housemounds that have been tested by excavation in Tikal and its vicinity, *not one* shows any hint of Eznab occupation. All of the Eznab debris comes from in and around palace structures. But the Eznab people were not living like the kings of yore, for the lack of maintenance had begun to tell, and on occasion roofs collapsed on the unhappy inhabitants of the rooms below. When this occurred, the debris was not even removed; if some sheltered space remained, the larger stones were shoved out of the way and occupation continued amidst the rubble. Instead of being swept and refreshed daily, as must have been the case in better days, courtyards, stairways, and even the corners of occupied rooms accumulated unsightly piles of garbage—a gold mine for archaeologists, but hardly up to centuries-old Maya standards of cleanliness. Like barbarians living untidily among the ruins of vanquished cities, the Eznab population survived for a time. But they were neither conquerors nor outsiders; they were, instead, the impoverished descendants who probably still recounted tales of the days of Maya glory. And not many were left to enjoy these tales, for I would calculate, from the number of rooms occupied, that the population of Tikal in Eznab times could have been no more than 10 percent of the total reached at the Imix peak less than a century earlier. The data are incontrovertible—the center of Tikal was decimated in a very short period of time, and construction and population suffered the same sudden and dramatic fate as calendric inscriptions.

One possibility remained, however, that might mitigate the scope of the disaster—the possibility that people simply abandoned the ceremonial centers and fled into the countryside. In a time of chaos when old leaders and old gods may be rejected, such a result might not be unexpected; for this reason several archaeologists have argued that the conclusion of a population disaster should not be too rapidly accepted. To put this idea to the test, the Tikal Sustaining Area Project investigated rural areas well away from the site center. A carefully designed research sample collected by Robert E. Fry demonstrated that the situation in the countryside was identical to that in the center—tiny Eznab population remnants in crumbling palaces and nobody at all in housemound areas. At Tikal, at least, the disaster was complete.

The survivors do not seem to have totally rejected the old ways, for although the construction of temples and carving of stelae ceased, there were attempts to continue pious practices. A very common phenomenon at Maya sites is what has been termed abnormal placement of stelae and altars. The Classic Maya had followed very strict rules for monuments: The monuments had to be grouped in sets that corresponded to certain sacred numbers; they could be put in some places but not in others; they had to be accompanied by very specific kinds of offerings. Sites as we find them today contain many monuments that violate these rules: unlucky-numbered sets; monuments in places that the Classic Maya would have found unthinkable; and monuments with either no offerings or offerings of the wrong kind. Barbarities such as broken stelae carefully set up, a couple so placed that the inscriptions are upside down, also occur. Careful excavation can usually demonstrate that abnormal monuments were pieces from earlier times that had been moved to new resting places very late in the history of sites where they are found. At Tikal, where abnormal placement has been exhaustively studied by Linton Satterwaite and William Coe, the results show that as many as 40 percent of the monuments in the area of the Great Plaza are aberrant late placements. Some of these placements certainly occurred in Eznab times; a few may have taken place even later. These aberrations look not so much like impiety as like efforts continue the stela cult by people who had lost the knowledge of the proper way of doing things.

Ceremonies continued in the temples as well, where the floors of rooms are littered with ashes and the remains of late types of incense burners—mute testimony to the continued feeling of sacredness that pervaded these holy places long after the high priests who first used them had ceased to exist. So ceremonial activity persisted in the simpler forms that were possible even after the maintenance of the great ceremonies and the experts in mystical matters had become an economic impossibility.

The Tikal of Eznab times was not a rejection of Maya patterns, but rather a Tikal gone poor; survivors carried on as they could, clinging to the same elite centers for living, and worshiping in the same sacred places. The best they could manage, however, was so impoverished that it became almost a parody of what once had been. Even these pitiful survivors, however, were unable to endure, and after a century and a half they, too, disappeared leaving Tikal empty and alone except for the teeming lesser life of the regenerating forest.

Other sites suggest that a wide area was similarly affected. At Uaxactun, near Tikal, Eznab-period debris covers palace floors and courtyards and occurs nowhere else, and stelae have been dragged hither and yon by late occupants. Similar things happened at San José in British Honduras and at Palenque and Piedras Negras on the Usumacinta River. The timing of events varied somewhat from site to site. Altar de Sacrificios and Seibal on the Pasion River to the south had heavy populations in times that are equivalent to Eznab, and Seibal carried out a vigorous program of elite construction while Tikal was probably already falling into ruin. But at these two sites the effect was only delayed, not avoided; a few years later they, too, were abandoned. A few sites may have escaped some of the effects of the collapse. Barton Ramie in Belize, for example, yields very late ceramic types that suggest a continued occupation at the site into times well after most known sites were completely abandoned.

Although it can be argued that data, particularly for rural areas, are still scanty, I think it extremely unlikely that anything yet to be discovered will change the conclusion that the Classic Maya of the southern lowlands suffered one of the world's great demographic disasters. Although total population estimates for the area have so little basis that I cannot even attempt to justify the figure, I feel that population loss may well have been in excess of a million people within a single century. A few people may have migrated out of the lowlands to surrounding areas, but there is no archaeological evidence that they did so, and there was no nearby area that could have begun to accommodate the total population that disappeared. The only conclusion is that a million or more Maya simply died.

Lest this interpretation conjure up garish pictures of streets and jungles piled high with rotting corpses, I should hasten to note that we are dealing with a period of four or five generations. It is an inescapable demographic fact that *all* of every population dies each generation, so the loss of a million Maya need not have been an overnight catastrophe. A far less spectacular but more likely mechanism of population loss can be generated by more subtle changes in birth and death rates. A decline in fertility and increases in death rates in crucial population segments such as young women or infants and children can work drastic changes in population totals over a period of several generations.

In its dying days, Classic Maya civilization was subject to pressures from new peoples outside the Classic tradition. The first indications of such people occur in late monuments carved just before the period of final crash. The influences are particularly strong at the site of Seibal on the Pasion River, where a spate of carving accompanied the late building surge mentioned earlier. Pictured on a number of Seibal stelae are strange people with waist-length hair and bone nose ornaments (Figure 33). Their appearance must have seemed outlandish by the standards of the times and was probably no better received than long hair in our own culture a few years ago. The newcomers may have been Maya—perhaps from some of the remote sections of the lowlands—but they certainly were not a part of the Classic Maya establishment. The long-hairs seem to have taken over leadership of Seibal, an event that may not have been well received, since some of the late architectural groups at the site seem to be arranged for easy defense. The take-over was re-

Figure 33

Seibal, Stela 3. *A number of late stelae from the site of Seibal depict people who are not like the Classic Maya. The long hair of this gentleman, reaching all the way to his feet, and the bone that he wears in his nose, are two features that distinguish this group of foreigners. (Courtesy of John A. Graham, University of California, Berkeley.)*

warded, at least for a time; Seibal population and construction continued to flourish for several decades after much of the low-lands was already in its decline. The dreadful malaise could not be avoided, however, and by the middle of the tenth century, Seibal, too, had become a wasteland.

Perhaps related to Seibal events, but more likely an inde-pendent influence, was a thrust into the lowlands that can be traced by the presence of pottery with very fine paste (usually of a ware called Fine Orange, but occurring also as Fine Gray and Fine Cream). Pottery of this kind is at home in the coastal lowlands of Vera Cruz and Tabasco northwest of the Maya low-lands, where pottery clay of an extremely fine, silty texture is available. Preliminary studies of trace elements indicate that the clay used for all of the fine paste pottery came from the same source. Thus the widespread occurrence of the pottery must be the result of trade. Fine paste pottery occurs earliest at sites along the Usumacinta River close to the Vera Cruz–Tabasco coastal plain. The pottery seems to have spread upriver (pre-sumably accompanied by human companions), and it became extremely abundant at the site of Altar de Sacrificios at the juncture of the Usumacinta and Pasion rivers. So much Fine Orange pottery occurs on the surface at Altar that Richard E. W. Adams feels that it must represent a brief final occupation by intruders from the fine paste homeland. At sites in the central lowlands like Tikal and Uaxactun, Fine Orange pottery was traded in in small quantities after Eznab peoples were already established.

A number of archaeologists, particularly those who have worked along the Pasion River, feel that the arrival of Fine Orange pottery was associated with an invasion of the lowlands that may have been a major factor in causing the Maya collapse. Others, including the present writer, feel that fine paste pottery arrived after the collapse and that intrusions of people from Vera Cruz and Tabasco are the *result* rather than the *cause* of the downfall. The disagreement can be resolved only by some very exacting work on chronology at a whole series of sites.

We have now, however, moved into the realm of causes and must consider several generations of attempts to explain what happened to the Maya. As soon as the facts of the Maya col-lapse became evident, archaeologists were attracted to the prob-lem and began to suggest reasons for it. The reasons advanced fall into several different categories. The first category may be called catastrophic, since it includes sudden, natural disasters that were beyond the control of Maya culture. Among catastro-phies suggested are earthquakes, climatic change, epidemics, and hurricanes. Earthquakes can be rejected as a likely cause, for there is no geological reason to believe that they have ever been severe in the Maya lowlands. Climatic change, disease, and hurricanes are still considered possible factors in the collapse of the system. A second major class of reasons may be termed ecological. Although varying in details, all ecological explanations share the idea that the Maya overpopulated and overfarmed their limited rain forest environment, with the result that their subsistence system failed. The thesis of overpopulation seems well justified, and subsistence failure remains a strong theme in present ideas about the collapse.

I will term the final class of explanations "social," since such explanations involve interaction within the social system rather than interaction between man and nature. The peasant revolt theory of J. Eric Thompson advances the idea that an increasingly burdensome exploitation of the lower class led to outright rebellion and destruction of the elite levels of society. Invasion hypotheses, already alluded to, would also be social explanations, since they attempt to explain the collapse as a result of conflict between the Maya and people outside the lowlands. Civil war hypotheses, based on the assumption that the Maya led to their own collapse by fighting among themselves, are similar. Other social explanations are trade hypotheses that suggest that the Maya collapse was triggered by a breakdown of long-distance trading systems. These explanations can, of course, be combined in a variety of ways, and there has been a tendency through time to move from single-cause theories to theories of a domino sort, in which a starting cause is seen as leading to a whole series of reactions that together resulted in the collapse.

For more than two generations archaeologists, in their attempts to understand the Maya collapse, based their efforts on a search for possible causes. A particular case would be advanced—invasion, for example—and argument would follow about whether or not the cause had occurred. Since data were usually not good enough to prove that the cause had or had not happened, or whether, if it had happened, it had preceded or followed the collapse, no real solutions could be achieved. In fact, articles about the collapse written in the late 1960s included almost nothing (except additional facts) that was not present in articles from the 1930s.

This was the context in which a group of specialists agreed in 1970 to meet at the School of American Research for a seminar specifically devoted to the problem of the Maya collapse. This seminar was a turning point in my own thinking and led to my approaching the problem in ways that are reflected

throughout this book. It was moreover, I feel, a milestone for Maya studies as a whole. The key to the formulation that
resulted was the realization that no explanation of the collapse of a social system can be achieved without a clear understanding of the way the system operated. This led us to reexamine Classic Maya culture and to challenge many previously held ideas about the Maya. The eventual model of the collapse that we achieved concentrates less upon "causes" like those listed above and more upon the stresses that were inherent in the very fabric of Late Classic Maya society.

In a summary article that draws together the ideas of all the participants of the Maya Collapse Seminar, Gordon R. Willey and Demitri B. Shimkin advance the idea that Late Classic Maya society was subject to a series of internal stresses that could only be worsened by a continuation of the very trends that had made the society successful. Most of these stresses have been discussed in previous chapters, but they must be brought together again to emphasize the complex ways in which they are interrelated.

Population was rising rapidly during the Maya Late Classic and would have increased demands for all commodities, but it would at the same time have supplied an increasing labor force. Since nutritional levels and sanitation—which can relate to checks on population growth—would have been better for the elite class than for commoners, it is not unlikely that elite levels of society were growing even more rapidly than lower levels.

Agricultural production would have been a point of stress at high population densities. Even if the Maya were still capable of expanding production by some of the means discussed in Chapter 4, such expansion must have been increasingly demanding in terms of the amount of labor it consumed. In addition, agriculture probably faced situations in which some of the techniques available for short-term expansion, such as decreasing the fallow cycle, may have presented risks of long-term deterioration of farming lands.

The *ability to respond to subsistence emergencies* would have been overtaxed by the stresses mentioned above. Even in relatively tolerant climates, crop losses occur from time to time and must be countered if disaster is to be avoided. Unless enough reserve food is stored locally to make up for temporary deficits, importation, which involves problems in trade and transportation, becomes necessary. High population and stress in the agricultural system would increase both the frequency and the magnitude of agricultural emergencies, which would then consume already critical weath and manpower supplies as well as increasing the competition between political units.

Malnutrition and *disease* were additional stress factors for the Maya. Malnutrition could result from stresses in the agricultural system that decreased either total food supply or the quantity of key dietary components such as protein. Disease was an ever-present possibility; many diseases, such as intestinal troubles of either bacterial or parasitic origin, were probably endemic in the Maya population. Malnutrition, if it occurred, could have raised the rates and severity of endemic diseases from levels quite acceptable for continued population survival to levels that would contribute to decline. Both malnutrition and disease would have the effect of reducing the labor output, thus potentially feeding the problem of an increasing shortage of labor back to the already stressed and labor-dependent agricultural system.

Competition between political units would increase as a result of increased population densities and consequent shortages of land and other resources. If competition took the form of warfare, additional stresses on all units would result, although a victorious power might temporarily improve its position at the expense of vanquished units. A more important, if more subtle, sort of competition was peaceful competition between centers for wealth and status (and associated economic advantages), which they would seek to achieve by lavish ceremonial displays, including the construction of even larger ceremonial centers. That investment in such competition was disastrously wasteful of manpower and resources and yielded no tangible returns may seem obvious to us, but there is no reason to think that the Maya so regarded it. Consumption in ceremonialism was part of a system that had worked well for many centuries. Centers that had excelled ceremonially had been rewarded by status and power and indirect benefits that contributed to their well-being. To expect a centuries-old system with demonstrated advantages to be dumped at a moment of stress would show little understanding of human conservatism or of the self-serving demands of power groups that become associated with any large system.

Increased investment in the elite levels of society would have been demanded at the same time that there were stresses at all levels. The fact that the elite class probably grew more rapidly than lower classes would have necessitated larger investments simply to maintain the *status quo*. Adding to this, increasing needs for competition among centers and expanding emergency facilities would have resulted in a rapid escalation of demands

upon those who supported the elite. Since the principal commodity that the lower classes have to contribute is labor
(whether expended in food production, crafts, or military service), the primary burden would have fallen upon manpower
supplies that were already under stress from other directions.

Management capabilities of the directorial class of Maya
society must have been severely stressed. Every increment of
expansion in the population and in the economic system would
have added to the tasks of record keeping, tax collection, and
transmission and enforcement of management directives. There
is no indication that Maya society attempted any major innovations in its managerial system, and it may have tried to get by
with methods suited only for a much smaller society.

The foregoing stress system is such that a difficulty in one
part of the interaction network can easily spread to cause difficulties in other parts, which then feed back to increase the
problem. Once this interconnection is obvious, the question of
cause becomes less interesting. Pressure or a minor crisis at any
of a number of sensitive points could set the entire cycle in
operation, and it is far more important to understand the way
in which the system reacted than to search for the starting
point of the reaction. In a sense, the reasons for the Maya
collapse are inherent in the system and are the same reasons
that for many centuries led to growth and success.

The final touch to an understanding of the Classic Maya
downfall can be added by turning to concepts from general
systems theory. Systems theory is a field that attempts to com-
prehend the properties of complex systems by stressing the
interrelationships between parts rather than by the more common practice of analyzing parts in isolation.

Complex systems are of many kinds. Some are extremely
stable and contain sets of regulatory (deviation-counteracting)
mechanisms that, by acting like thermostats in a heating system,
keep variables such as population, economics, and so on, close
to steady values. Other systems are growth systems, in which
parts are connected by growth (deviation-amplifying) loops in
which an increase in one part causes an increase in a second
part, which feeds back to cause further increase in the first
part, and so on *ad infinitum*.

The continual expansion of the Maya—in population, in size
and number of sites, and in complexity—shows all the characteristics of a growth system. So far so good; this concept may
help us to understand Maya development up to the time of the
Late Classic, but what does it have to do with the collapse?
To clarify this part of the problem, it is necessary to introduce

another property of growth systems—the overshoot mode. No system can grow indefinitely, since if it did, it would eventually absorb all the energy and matter in the universe. Consequently, growing systems meet one of two fates. Some reach equilibrium; growth slows and eventually ceases, and the system becomes a stable system in which further change is minimal. Other systems, rather than achieving equilibrium, outgrow their resources and "overshoot." When this happens, many of the same cycles that caused growth reverse themselves and the system declines. A simple example may help to illustrate the concept. Consider the expansion of a city into a new area. People begin to move into the area and soon, because of the population, businesses and industries are attracted. Jobs from business and industry attract more people, who attract more business and so on. Eventually, however, as the area becomes older and more crowded, some people (usually well-to-do members of the community) begin to move out to other new areas. With loss of some wealth, businesses may begin to close or move elsewhere, further weakening the economic and population base, and the whole cycle may accelerate in the new (and opposite) direction. This is a case of overshoot, and the result can be downward revision to a point at which growth may start over again.

I feel that the Maya collapse is an exemplary case of overshoot by a culture that had expanded too rapidly and had used its resources recklessly in an environment that demanded careful techniques of conservation. The Maya outran their resource base, not only in terms of farming capabilities, but also in terms of organizational capabilities, the ability to distribute goods, and the ability to use manpower efficiently. Growth cycles reversed, and the resource base was so badly overstrained that the cycle of decline for the Maya could not be stopped, short of the final resting point of near depopulation. The ravaged land offered little potential for repopulation, and the rain forest home of the Maya still remains an unpopulated wilderness with only the silent remains of the vast temple centers to remind the visitor of its once great past.

Are the Maya simply an historical curiosity of concern only to those with an antiquarian passion for the strange and long-forgotten? A few years ago even many of those involved in Maya studies might have agreed that such was the case. But if the analysis that the Maya were victims of overshoot in a growth cycle is correct, their relevance to the present may be far greater. Recently a group of scientists from the Club of Rome, an informal organization of experts concerned with the future environment of our planet, simulated the future of the world by computer techniques. The results reported in *The Limits to Growth* are sobering indeed. The near future, like the recent past, inevitably holds unprecedented world population growth and economic expansion as well as rapidly accelerating use of natural resources and generation of the pollutants associated with technology. Then the skyrocketing curves of growth level off and begin to turn downward, at first slowly and then in an ever-accelerating cycle of decline that stabilizes only after it has reached very low levels. The computer curves are easy to interpret but hard to accept. If they are correct, a frightening percentage of the world's population faces extinction in the next few centuries. There is no guarantee, of course, that the computer projections are correct and many reputable scientists have raised objections about the data and methods involved. Worldwide data are extremely difficult to assemble with any pretense at accuracy; computer simulations demand a series of shaky assumptions; it is next to impossible to make allowance in projections for possible breakthroughs in technology. We can certainly argue about the accuracy of projections about the future, but we ignore them only at our peril.

At this point, we can close the circle to the Maya once again. The curves that we could estimate for the Maya rise and decline would look very much like the Club of Rome's computer simulations of the modern world. If we ourselves stand at the edge of a precipice—our entire world endangered by the possibility of a global overshoot—can we say any longer that the fact that the Maya overpopulated, overexploited their environment, and disappeared from the earth bears no relationship to modern problems? Instead, should we not ask whether the knowledge and information we can glean from a study of the Maya failure can be applied to our own situation? Given an understanding of the forces that destroyed earlier civilizations, can we not look at ourselves and our society and marshal our talents and energies in a determined effort to avoid a world collapse—a collapse from which there might be no return for the human race?

Selected Readings

The following list of titles has been developed for the nonprofessional reader who may wish to find out more about the Maya. Most of the books suggested are still in print; those that are not should be available in most university libraries.

Coe, Michael D.

1966 *The Maya.* New York: Praeger, Ancient Peoples and Places Series. A good summary for the general reader.

Culbert, T. Patrick (Editor)

1973 *The Classic Maya Collapse.* Albuquerque: University of New Mexico Press. The first book to present the new view of the Maya utilized here. Theoretical and data articles, some quite technical. Extensive bibliography.

Greene, Merle, and J. E. S. Thompson

1967 *Ancient Maya Relief Sculpture.* New York: Museum of Primitive Art. A beautiful book of rubbings made from Maya sculptures. Short introduction and descriptions of each sculpture.

Greene, Merle, Robert L. Rands, and John A. Graham

1972 *Maya Sculpture.* Berkeley: Lederer, Street and Zeus. More than 400 pages of magnificent rubbings of Maya sculptures, accompanied by short descriptions.

Morley, Sylvanus G., revised by George W. Brainerd

1956 *The Ancient Maya,* 3rd ed. Stanford: Stanford University Press. A standard source on the Maya. Now out of date in many ways but still good for descriptions of sites and information on calendrics and carved monuments.

Proskouriakoff, Tatiana

1963 *An Album of Maya Architecture.* Norman: University of Oklahoma Press. A series of gorgeous reproduction drawings of the way Maya sites and structures would have looked at the time they were in use.

Stephens, John L.

1841   (reprint 1969) *Incidents of Travel in Central America, Chiapas and Yucatan*, 2 vols. New York: Dover.

1843   (reprint 1962) *Incidents of Travel in Yucatan*. Norman: University of Oklahoma Press. The travel accounts that excited nineteenth-century America and reintroduced Maya civilization. Still good reading.

Thompson, J. E. S.

1963   *Maya Archaeologist*. Norman: University of Oklahoma Press. An exciting account of the author's adventures during a career devoted to Maya archaeology.

1966   *The Rise and Fall of Maya Civilization*, 2nd ed. Norman: University of Oklahoma Press. An excellent general summary of the prehistoric Maya. Highly readable and sensitive to the Maya way of life.

1971   *Maya Hieroglyphic Writing: An Introduction*, new edition. Norman: University of Oklahoma Press. The basic book on Maya hieroglyphics and calendrics. Well written, but heavy going because of the subject matter.

Tozzer, Alfred M. (Editor)

1941   "Landa's Relacion de las Cosas de Yucatan," *Papers of the Peabody Museum of Archaeology and Ethnology*, vol. 18. Cambridge, Mass.: Harvard University Press. An English translation of Bishop Landa's account of the Conquest period Maya, accompanied by useful explanatory notes.

INDEX

Page numbers in italics denote illustrations.

76 77 9 8 7 6 5 4